Pop-Up Cards

Pop-Up Cards

and other greetings that slide, dangle & move

with Sandi Genovese

LARK BOOKS
A Division of Sterling Publishing Co., Inc.
New York / London

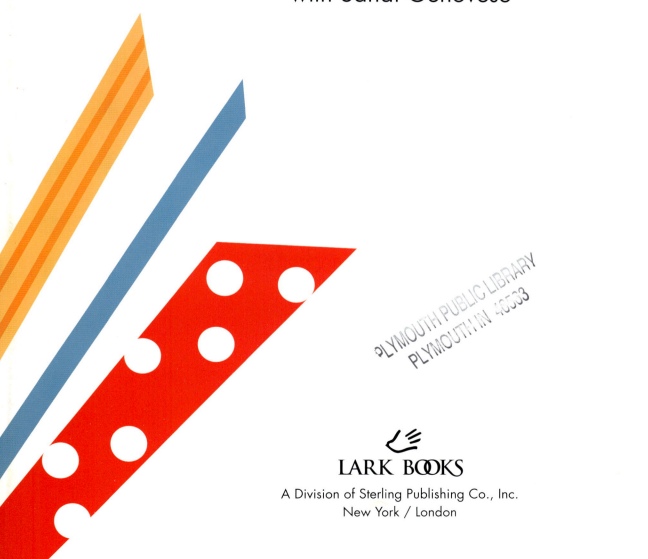

A Red Lips 4 Courage Communications, Inc., book

www.redlips4courage.com

Eileen Cannon Paulin, *President*

Catherine Risling, *Director of Editorial*

Book Editor: Lecia Monsen

Copy Editors: Lisa Anderson, Catherine Risling

Book Designer: Jeffrey Hill

Photographer: Zachary Williams

Stylist: Rebecca Ittner

Library of Congress Cataloging-in-Publication Data

Genovese, Sandi.

Pop-up cards and other greetings that slide, dangle & move / with Sandi Genovese. – 1st edi.

p. cm.

Includes index.

ISBN-13: 978-1-60059-226-3 (hc-plc with jacket : alk. paper)

ISBN-10: 1-60059-226-0 (hc-plc with jacket : alk. paper)

1. Greeting cards. I. Title.

TT872.G46 2008

745.594'1–dc22

2007046183

Published by Lark Books, A Division of Sterling Publishing Co., Inc.

387 Park Avenue South, New York, NY 10016

Distributed in Canada by Sterling Publishing, c/o Canadian Manda Group, 165 Dufferin Street Toronto, Ontario, Canada M6K 3H6

Distributed in the United Kingdom by GMC Distribution Services, Castle Place, 166 High Street, Lewes, East Sussex, England BN7 1XU

Distributed in Australia by Capricorn Link (Australia) Pty Ltd., P.O. Box 704, Windsor, NSW 2756 Australia

If you have questions or comments about this book, please contact:

Lark Books

67 Broadway

Asheville, NC 28801

(828) 253-0467

Manufactured in China

ISBN 13: 978-1-60059-226-3

ISBN 10: 1-60059-226-0

For information about custom editions, special sales, premium and corporate purchases, please contact Sterling Special Sales Department at (800) 805-5489 or specialsales@sterlingpub.com.

Contents

Introduction

It all began more than twenty-five years ago, when I decided to make my own holiday cards. The very first card was an ornament I made from the plastic lid of a potato salad container decorated with colored markers and shrunk in the oven. I added a seasonal greeting and ribbon to hang the card. Ever since then, I have designed my own greeting cards and my friends and family have begun calling them Sandi Cards.

So what is a "Sandi Card?" It folds flat for mailing but usually becomes three-dimensional when opened. Often it's interactive, with parts that slide or move in order to view the message. Other times, some simple assembly may be required.

I have discovered that people enjoy interacting with the cards. They also like to assemble the pieces as long as it's not too difficult. It's not unusual for my cards to come with a few sentences explaining the assembly or, more often, a simple drawing that shows the card in its finished state. When the holidays are over, the cards are usually saved and displayed the following year.

Once my friends were spoiled with handmade cards during the holidays they came to expect them for other special events throughout the year. I realized that it was easy to adapt the designs to all sorts of seasons and occasions by simply changing the colors and theme of the embellishments. You will find that you can do the same thing with the cards in this book, so don't be discouraged if the projects are not themed for your needs. Use the pattern provided to cut out the card base, but change the colors, embellishments, and greetings to make the card your own.

Sandi

Card Basics

Card Basics

I believe that making a card for someone special is time well spent, and you need not break the bank to do it.

I purposely made the projects in this book using the most basic tools and materials. If you have a paper trimmer or even a pair of scissors, an assortment of circle and shape punches, and paper or cardstock packs with two or three shades of each color, you are ready to make these cards.

The embellishments I used include punched elements, die cuts, and stickers. Sometimes I simply drew the decorative elements by hand. Regardless of theme or occasion, you shouldn't have trouble finding items to fit your desired card. Patterns are provided to make the creation of the card base easy, but I hope you will be inspired to play with the embellishments and really personalize your cards, making them as unique as the lucky recipients.

USING OPTIONAL TOOLS

I simply fold my cards by hand but you can use an embossing stylus to draw the crease line and then reinforce the fold with a bone folder.

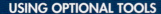

COMMON TOOLS & MATERIALS

I use many of these tools and materials in most of the projects in this book. It's good to collect these basic items before beginning a project so that you don't have to go looking for the right marker or paper punch in the middle of creating a card.

- Bone folder*
- Computer and printer
- Craft knife
- Craft scissors
- Cutting mat
- Die-cut machine with dies
- Embossing stylus*
- Fine-point markers
  black, red, silver, white
- Hole punches
- Paper
  cardstock (110 lb.)
  decorative (scrapbook)
  heavyweight paper (92 lb.)
- Paper punches in various shapes and sizes
- Paper trimmer
- Pencil
- Ruler
- Thread

**optional*

DIMENSIONAL CARD FORMATS

Sliders and pop ups—are we talking baseball or card making? The three-dimensional cards in this book can be described in many ways, but I call them accordions, dangles, animations, and ones that require a little assembly. The beauty of creating a dimensional card, believe it or not, is its simplicity. The patterns provided make it easy to create the card base that is responsible for the "wow" appeal of the cards. Adding embellishments and a greeting will finish the card and establish its theme. The projects are organized into the following categories:

POP-UPS

Pop-up cards involve cutting and folding tabs, allowing the embellishments inside to spring right off the card. The number, size, and placement of the tabs can vary, but the construction of mine generally follows this guide: vertical lines are cut and horizontal lines are folded. The only exception to this is the *Have Your Cake* card on pages 17–19. Whether the pop-ups are horizontal or vertical, a cover is needed to conceal the notches that are visible at the back of the card where each tab is cut.

ACCORDIONS

Accordion cards involve fan-folding paper or cardstock into pleats. The pleats can vary in number and size and can be made horizontally or vertically. The pleats fold up fairly flat when the card is closed but will spread out when opened to reveal several layers of design.

DANGLE

Dangle cards have one or more elements suspended so that they hang down and are visible through an opening in the card. Thread is sandwiched between a pair of matching shapes such as die cuts, punched shapes, or mirror-image stickers to create the hanging elements that are taped to the back of the card.

SOME ASSEMBLY REQUIRED

Some of my favorite cards need to be assembled by the recipient. My friends tell me that they enjoy the challenge of figuring out a little simple assembly. If I think it may be too difficult, I will include a sketch of what the card looks like assembled, and that seems to be enough to ensure successful card assembly along with the pleasure that comes from the interaction with the card.

ANIMATION

Animated cards have some kind of movement inherent in the design. One example of this is the slider card, which has a panel that slides to reveal a hidden message. The center section of a flip-flop card moves back and forth as the card is opened and closed. Other card's contents jump from the left side to the right and back, depending on which way the cover is opened.

GREETINGS

My greetings are combinations of stickers, rub ons, computer printouts, rubber stamped, or handwritten words.

It's up to you to pick the method that suits you. Sometimes it's fun to combine more than one method on a card. Try changing the colors and theme of the embellishments along with the greeting for a different occasion altogether.

IN OTHER WORDS . . .

You will see this tip box throughout the book. It will contain alternative greetings that you might select for some of the cards.

Once the base has been created it is simply a matter of embellishing the card. You can follow the directions to create a card that looks like mine or choose different embellishments and do your own thing. Your embellishments can be as elaborate as you want. Most times I kept it simple by relying on stickers, die cuts, punches, or cutting them by hand.

The themes of my embellishments are pretty basic and it should be easy to locate similar decorations. Feel free to substitute or interchange different elements whenever you can't find the embellishment that matches mine or when you want to explore your own creativity.

PATTERNS

Patterns are provided for the cards to make it easy to master the three-dimensional card formats. Enlarge the pattern on a photocopier and use it to mark the fold and cut lines on each card. A solid black line is a cut line. A blue line indicates a mountain fold and a red line refers to a valley fold. When a cut line is indicated on the interior of the card, you will need to use a craft knife.

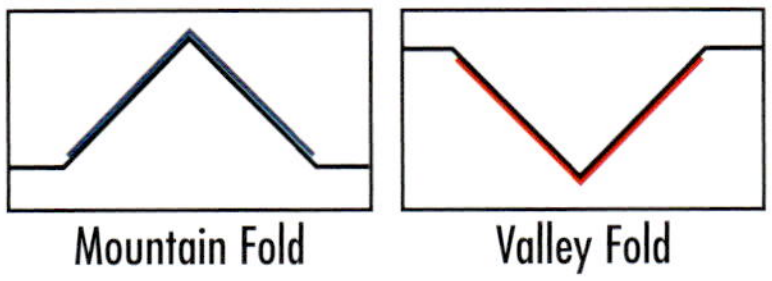

ADHESIVES

- Adhesive roller — I use an adhesive roller almost exclusively because it's easy to use and eliminates the paper puckering that wet craft glue can cause.
- Cellophane tape — When I need to attach a hanging element to a card, I use this clear tape to secure the thread to the paper.
- Foam adhesive — I use foam adhesive to hold embellishments when I want to add extra dimension to a project.
- Glue dots — Because of their strong holding power, I use glue dots on projects when items need additional reinforcement, are heavy, or are in an area of the card that will be handled repeatedly.

ENVELOPES

You can find envelopes in lots of colors and sizes in paper, craft, or scrapbook stores or online. You can also make your own.

There is an envelope pattern for all of the cards in this book, but you can also recycle a used envelope and turn it into a pattern. Place the envelope in the freezer until the glue loses its grip. Open the envelope and use it as a guide to make your own envelope. If you want to create a different size envelope, slice the pattern down the middle and overlap the trimmed edges to make it smaller, or pull it apart to make it larger.

A vertical cut adjusts the width and a horizontal cut modifies the length of the envelope. Tape it together once you're satisfied with the size and then trace it onto a large piece of paper.

Coordinate the colors and patterns of the envelope with the card it will hold for an envelope that is as customized as the card itself.

ENVELOPE SIZES

A variety of envelopes are used throughout this book. Some are available for purchase at craft stores and others you will need to make using the patterns provided. The sizes of envelopes used are:

#10 (letter-size)—4⅛" x 9½" (10.5 x 24 cm)
A6—4¾" x 6½" (12.1 x 17.6 cm)
A7—5¼" x 7¼" (13.3 x 18.4 cm)
A10—6" x 9" (15.2 x 22.9 cm)
3¾" x 7" (9.5 x 17.8 cm)
5¾" (14.6 cm) square
6" (15.2 cm) square
6" x 7" (15.2 x 17.8 cm)
6¼" x 8" (15.8 x 20.3 cm)
7¾" x 7" (19.7 x 17.8 cm)
7 ⅝" x 8" (19.9 x 20.3 cm)
8" (20.3 cm) square
9¼" x 6¼" (23.5 x15.8 cm)

Projects

Make Some Noise

Create the look of a party with a card featuring confetti and party blowers that are popping out all over. This card format creates a symmetrical pattern that reminds me of bowling pins. It's perfect for tall, thin embellishments like these party blowers.

TOOLS & MATERIALS

- A7 envelope
- Adhesive roller
- Craft knife
- Craft scissors
- Foam adhesive
- Paper: assorted colors and patterns (7–8), black, black-and-white checked, red, white
- Pencil
- Ruler
- Stickers: birthday greeting, various colored strips

HOW-TO

CREATE THE CARD

1. Trace the card onto white paper (see Pattern 19, page 112) and cut it out. Cut the cover ¼" (.06 cm) larger than the card from red paper.

2. Using a craft knife, cut the slits and then fold on the crease lines. Adhere the card to the cover, avoiding adhesive behind each pop-up tab.

Make Some Noise

EMBELLISH THE CARD

3. Cut out the party blowers freehand from assorted colors of paper and add details from printed and plain papers. Fasten one embellishment to each pop-up tab and add a triple mat using red, black-and-white checked, and black papers to the bottom for the greeting. Cut colored sticker strips into bits to sprinkle across the inside of the card as confetti.

DECORATE THE COVER

4. Decorate the cover with a wide white border and black-and-white checked band. Cut a black rectangle large enough to hold the birthday greeting sticker, some confetti pieces, and part of an additional party blower. Center and adhere the embellished piece to the cover with foam adhesive.

IN OTHER WORDS . . .

- Celebrate!
- Happy Birthday
- May All Your Wishes Come True

Have Your Cake

This style of pop-up card features horizontal slits with vertical crease lines. A graduated series of slits results in a shape that can be decorated to resemble a birthday cake, wedding cake, Christmas tree, or any other tall, triangular-shaped object. If you want to experiment, change the triangle format to a diamond, oval, or other geometric shape and see what other ideas you can come up with.

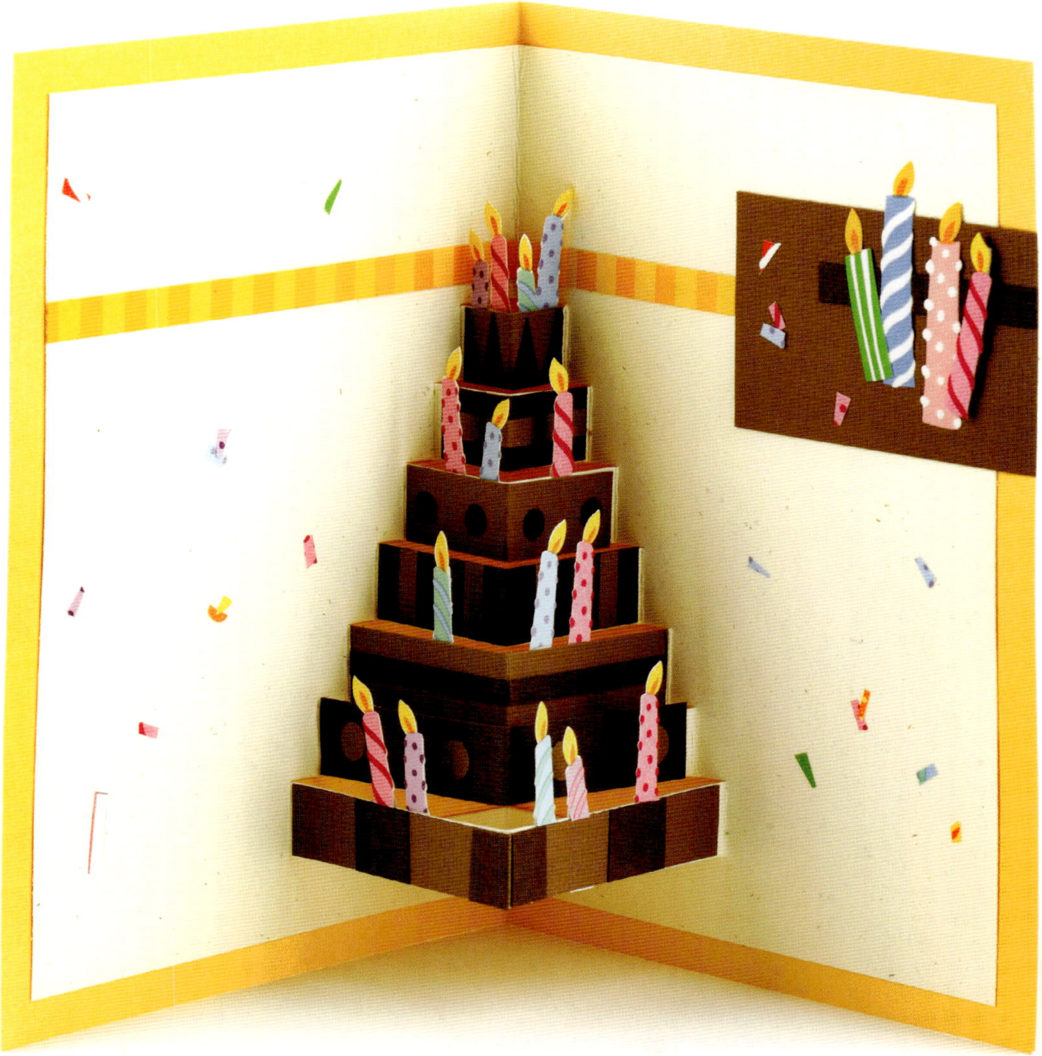

Have Your Cake

TOOLS & MATERIALS

- A6 envelope
- Adhesive roller
- Cardstock: cream, dark brown, light brown, yellow
- Circle punches: $\frac{1}{8}$" (0.3 cm), $\frac{1}{4}$" (0.6 cm)
- Craft knife
- Craft scissors
- Foam adhesive
- Paper: yellow checked
- Pencil
- Ruler
- Stickers: mirror-image candles

HOW-TO

CREATE THE CARD

1. Trace the card base onto cream cardstock (see Pattern 9, page 105) and cut it out. Using a craft knife, cut the slits and then fold on the crease lines.

2. Add candle stickers randomly to every other tier of the cake. Back each candle with a mirror-image sticker to eliminate exposed adhesive and to prevent the candles from sticking to the card when closed.

3. Embellish the cake tiers with two shades of brown cardstock. Create dots using circle punches and then add stripes, checks, and triangles to each tier with an adhesive roller.

4. Cut a $\frac{1}{4}$" (0.6 cm) yellow checked paper strip and adhere it horizontally along the top of the card. Cut and adhere $1\frac{1}{2}$" x $2\frac{1}{2}$" (3.8 x 6.4 cm) rectangle of light brown cardstock to the upper right side of the card and embellish it with $\frac{1}{4}$" (0.6 cm) strip of dark brown cardstock and candle stickers.

5. Cut a few candle stickers into tiny pieces to sprinkle as confetti on the inside of the card.

CREATE THE COVER

6. Measure and cut a card cover ½" (1.3 cm) larger than the card from yellow cardstock. Attach the card to the cover, avoiding the back of the cake tiers.

7. Cut a 2¼" x 4½" (5.7 x 11.4 cm) light brown stripe and mat it with cream cardstock. Cut a ½" x 4½" (1.3 x 11.4 cm) dark brown stripe and adhere it onto the middle of the light brown piece. Add candle stickers to the top of the matted piece, raising some with foam adhesive. Adhere the matted piece to the cover.

ADAPTING TO DIFFERENT OCCASIONS

The birthday cake can be re-invented as a wedding or anniversary cake simply by changing the colors and embellishments—or do a complete makeover and change the cake to a tree for a holiday card.

Time Stands Still

Time flies when you're having fun making a card like this. Customize your card even more with watchbands that represent the recipient's style. The "wow" factor on this card is great, but the skill required is minimal because most of the embellishments can be cut with a paper trimmer and circle punches. Try it for a guaranteed good time. The inside greeting reads "Enjoy Your Free Time."

TOOLS & MATERIALS

- 6¼" x 8" (15.8 x 20.3 cm) envelope
- Adhesive roller
- Cardstock: black, blue
- Craft knife
- Craft scissors
- Fine-point markers: black, silver
- Foam adhesive
- Paper: assorted blues (2), assorted colors (3–4), black, white
- Paper punches: assorted sizes
- Pencil
- Ruler

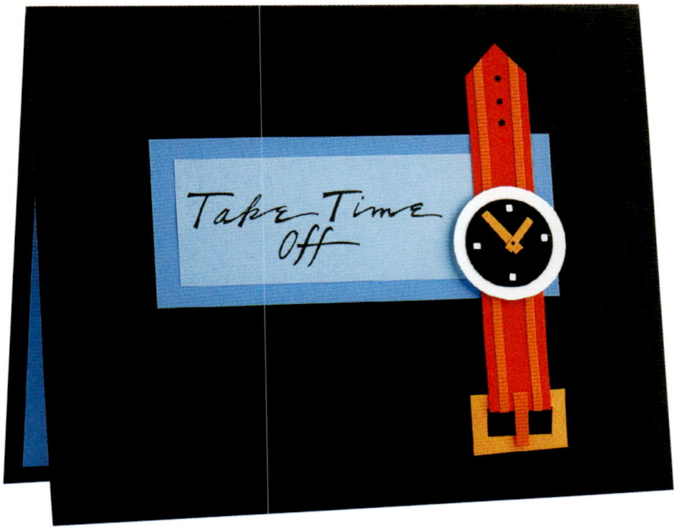

HOW-TO

CREATE THE CARD

1. Trace the pop-up card onto blue cardstock (see Pattern 7, page 104) and cut it out. Cut the cover ½" (1.3 cm) larger from black cardstock. Using a craft knife, cut the slits and then fold on the crease lines to create five pop-up tabs. Adhere the card and cover together using the adhesive roller.

2. *To create watches:* Cut the watch faces from black or white paper in various-sized circles, squares, and rectangles using paper punches and scissors. Mat each watch face with a contrasting color. Add symbols on the watch faces with markers using dots, numbers, or roman numerals. Add the hour and minute hands in assorted paper colors.

Time Stands Still

EMBELLISH THE CARD

3. Cut the watchband strips in different widths that correspond to their respective watch face. Use patterned paper or add details with contrasting colored circles and stripes. Allow extra length on each watchband to wrap around the buckle section of the watch.

4. *To create a buckle:* Cut out a rectangle ¼" (.06 cm) wider than the watchband. Cut out the inside of the rectangle to accommodate the band's width. Cut a narrow paper strip for the buckle's tongue and adhere it to the outside of the watchband and buckle.

5. Double-mat two shades of blue paper for the greeting and add an extra watch face, secured with foam adhesive.

6. Center and adhere the embellished blue double mat on the card's cover.

IN OTHER WORDS . . .

- It's about Time . . . We Got Together!
- Time is Precious . . . So Are You
- Time Flies . . . When You're Having Fun
- When I'm with You . . . Time Stands Still

Bunches of Good Wishes

Bring a little of the outdoors inside with a card that is literally popping with flowers. The beauty of flowers is their versatility—this card works well for many themes including thank you, friendship, or springtime. The graphic design of these flowers is simple enough for anyone to create—begin with a hand-drawn circle and go a little crazy.

Bunches of Good Wishes

TOOLS & MATERIALS

- A6 envelope
- Adhesive roller
- Circle punches: assorted sizes
- Craft knife
- Craft scissors
- Fine-point marker: black
- Foam adhesive
- Paper: assorted greens (2–3), black, blues (2), colors for flowers, red, white
- Pencil
- Ruler
- Sticker sentiment

HOW-TO

CREATE THE CARD

1. Trace the pop-up card onto white paper (see Pattern 8, page 104) and cut it out. Cut the card cover from the darker blue paper ½" (1.3 cm) larger than the card.

2. Using a craft knife, cut the slits and then fold on the crease lines, creating eight pop-up tabs. Attach the pop-up card to the cover using the adhesive roller and avoiding the pop-up tabs.

CREATE THE FLOWERS

3. For each flower, cut two or three layers of wobbly shaped circles in graduated sizes. Cut several freehand leaves and stems for each flower from green papers. Replicate the look of a vein in the leaf with a strip of contrasting green paper. Repeat to create nine flowers.

4. Adhere a stem, leaves, and flower to each pop-up tab. Be sure to check the height of the flower on the tab before adhering it so it doesn't peek out of the closed card.

CREATE THE LADYBUG

5. Punch one circle from both red and black papers. Cut a wide pie slice out of the red circle. Adhere the black circle to the backside of the red circle so it fills the pie slice and forms the head. Draw the wings and embellish them with black dots using a marker. Add the ladybug to the card using foam adhesive. Print or write a sentiment on white paper and mat it with black paper. Adhere the matted piece to the inside of the card.

EMBELLISH THE COVER

6. Decorate the cover with the sticker sentiment, double-matted in two shades of blue. Add an additional flower adhered with foam adhesive and flank with two green leaves as the finishing touch.

IN OTHER WORDS . . .

- Thanks . . . a Bunch
- Take Time . . . to Smell the Flowers
- Spring has Sprung
- Flower Power

VARIATION

The same pop-up design can be used for cards for many occasions by simply changing die-cut shapes and the greeting. Throughout the book I will share ideas for variations for other celebrations. Here, some of the stars are cut from patterned paper and some are rubber-stamped using a fresh pencil eraser and an inkpad for a dotted star. Others are decorated using strips of paper for a striped star. You can hand write the information, print it using a computer, or rubber stamp it—whatever suits your personal style.

Hand in Hand

Replicate the look of lots of hands clapping with an accordion-pleated card that is sure to generate applause. This card is meant to be viewed vertically. When the hands are attached to the front of some pleats and the back of others, it creates the look of hands clapping when the card is opened and closed.

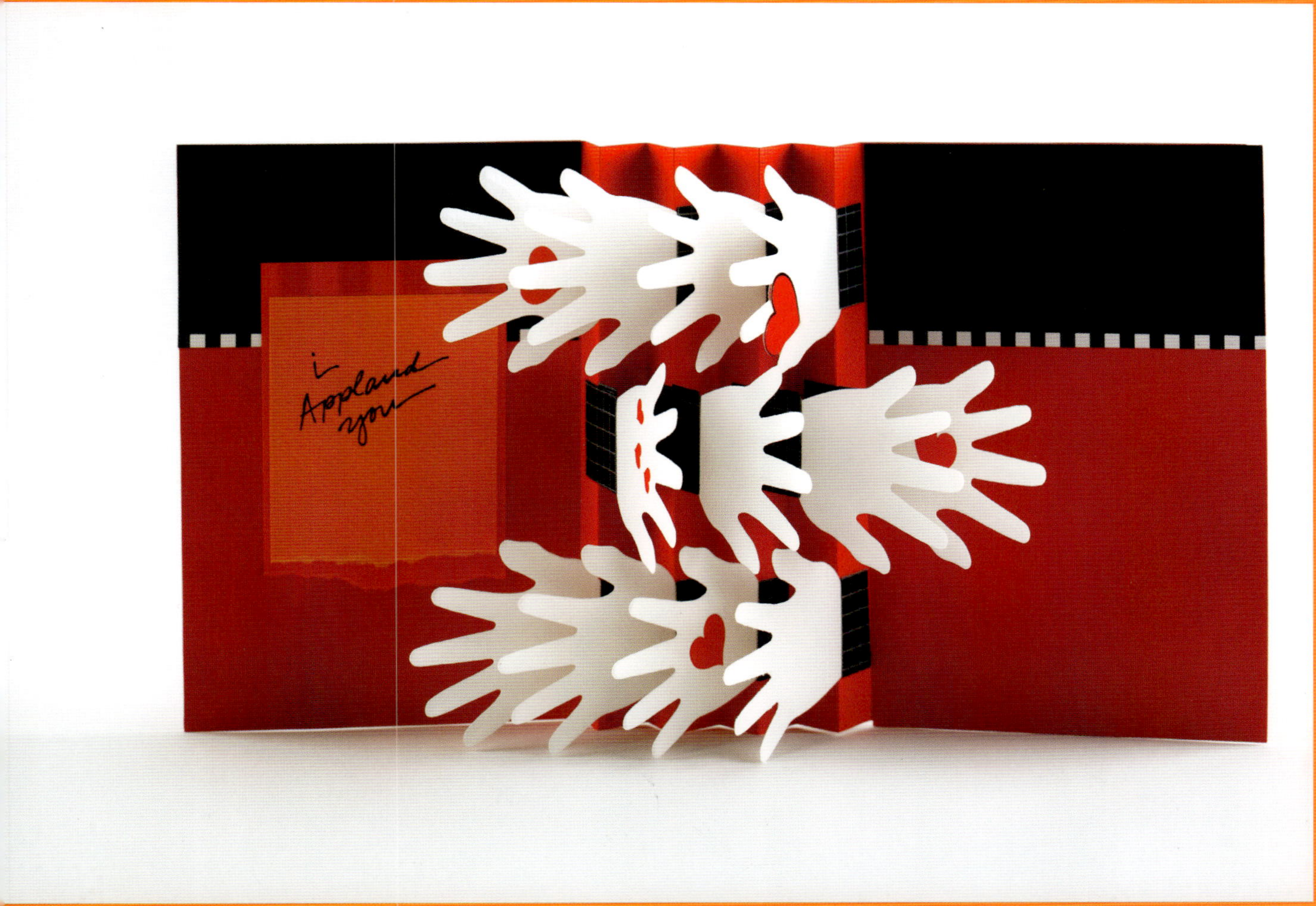

Hand in Hand

TOOLS & MATERIALS

- A6 envelope
- Adhesive roller
- Circle punch
- Craft scissors
- Die cuts: white hand (13)
- Embroidery floss: red
- Paper: black, black-and-white checked, black grid, orange, red, yellow
- Pencil
- Stickers: various-sized red hearts

HOW-TO

CREATE THE CARD

1. Trace the card onto red paper (see Pattern 4, page 100) and cut it out. Accordion-fold on the crease lines, resulting in a front and back cover with four pleats in the middle.

EMBELLISH THE CARD

2. Make shirt cuffs for nine hand die cuts from black grid paper cut slightly longer than the wrist. Increase the cuff width from ¼" (0.6 cm) to ½" (1.3 cm) for four additional hands. Adhere the cuffs to the hands with adhesive roller. Embellish a few hands with red heart stickers as desired.

3. Attach each set of four hands that form the top and bottom rows to the backside of each pleat with adhesive roller. The middle row of four hands with taller cuffs is attached to the front side of each pleat. *Note: Cuffs are taller in the middle row to elevate hands so they won't catch on other rows of hands. If you make your card taller or your hands smaller you won't need to do this.* Reserve the remaining hand for the card cover.

4. Adhere a wide black paper border and black-and-white checked strip to the top of each inside cover. Add a double mat embellished with colored squares and a torn paper bottom to the inside of the front cover to feature the greeting.

DECORATE THE COVER

5. Adhere a wide black border, black-and-white checked strip, and polka dots made with a circle punch on the outside front cover. Finish the card with the remaining hand. Add a tiny heart sticker as a button to the cuff. Cut a simple tag out of orange paper and hang it from one finger with embroidery floss.

IN OTHER WORDS...

- Good Friends & Good Times . . . Go Hand in Hand
- Hi "Hand"some . . . You're So Handy
- Congrats! . . . A Round of Applause for a Good Job!

Go Fish

There is so much drama in opening a card to reveal rows and rows of embellishments. In this project I decorated each accordion pleat with waves that are jumping with fish but it's easy to substitute other elements for the waves and fish in order to change the theme of the card. Give a card like this and you're sure to make a big splash!

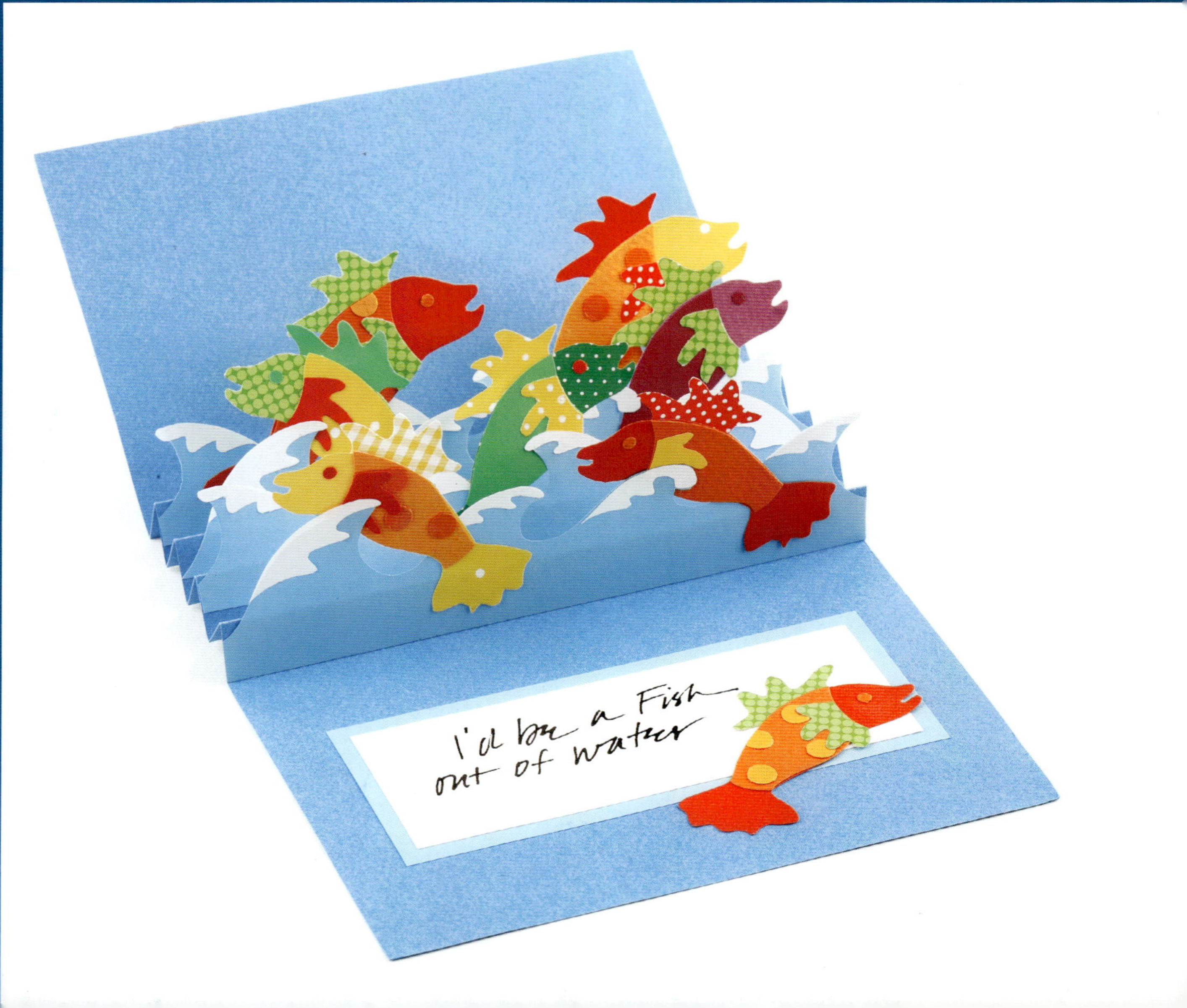

TOOLS & MATERIALS

- A6 envelope
- Adhesive roller
- Craft scissors
- Paper: assorted colors and patterns, light blue, medium blue, swirl patterns, white
- Pencil
- Stickers: letters

HOW-TO

CREATE THE CARD

1. Trace the card onto medium blue paper (see Pattern 4, page 100) and cut it out. Accordion-fold on the crease lines, resulting in a front and back cover with multiple pleats in the middle.

Go Fish

EMBELLISH THE CARD

2. Cut five wave strips from light blue and white papers. Trim the white waves to create whitecaps and adhere to the blue wave strips. Fasten a wave strip to each accordion pleat, alternating each wave's direction.

3. Cut several fish from an assortment of plain and patterned colored papers. Mix and match portions of each to create fish with a rainbow of embellishments like fins and tails and everything in between. Attach a fish to each wave strip. *Note: I drew my fish by hand but you can use stickers, die cuts, or rubber-stamped designs if you're not comfortable drawing them.*

4. Double-mat white and blue paper for the inside greeting and decorate it with an additional fish.

5. Decorate the cover with bands of colored paper, a wave strip, and a jumping fish.

6. Add a greeting to the bottom panel using stickers.

IN OTHER WORDS . . .

- Thank You . . . Your Thoughtfulness Made a Big Splash
- Don't Worry . . . There are More Fish in the Sea
- Goin' Fishin' . . . Enjoy Your Retirement

A Tree-Mendous Holiday

This card is a real "treet" for your friends and family. Once opened, it makes a grand holiday display but folds flat to be stored until next year. Now that's a card that keeps on giving. It's surprisingly simple to make, demonstrating how even the most basic supplies can be used to create a tree-mendous card.

A Tree-Mendous Holiday

TOOLS & MATERIALS

- A6 envelope
- Adhesive roller
- Craft scissors
- Fine-point marker: red, silver
- Foam adhesive
- Hole punch
- Paper: green (2 shades), metallic gold, red, white
- Pencil
- Ruler
- Stickers: mirror-image stars

HOW-TO

CREATE THE CARD

1. Trace the card onto red paper (see Pattern 4, page 100) and cut it out. Accordion-fold on the crease lines.

EMBELLISH INTERIOR

2. Cut eleven 2" x 4" (5.1 x 10.2 cm) rectangles from white paper and eleven from green paper. Trim all of the rectangles into triangles. Randomly punch holes in all the white trees and adhere them on top of the green trees.

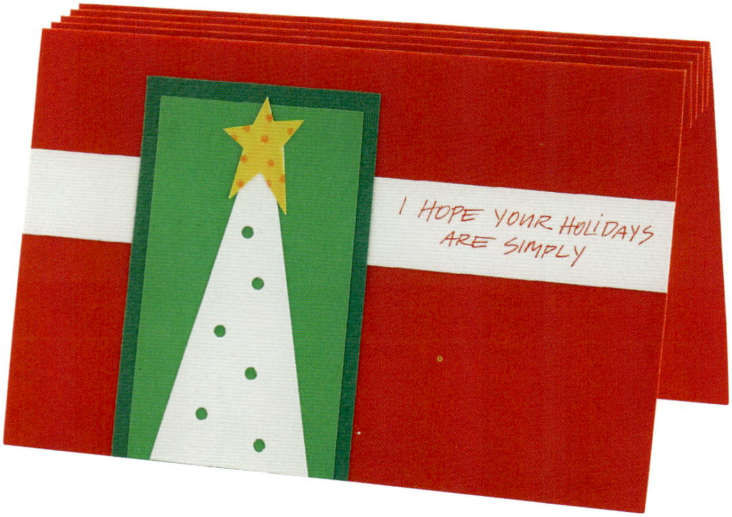
I HOPE YOUR HOLIDAYS
ARE SIMPLY

3. Adhere ten trees onto the fronts of the pleats—two trees to the first pleat, three to the next pleat—using the adhesive roller. Repeat with the remaining trees and pleats.

4. Attach the star stickers to some trees with the mirror-image stickers on the backside.

5. Trim ¾" (1.9 cm) from the bottom of the remaining tree. Cut a ¾" x 1" (1.9 x 2.5 cm) trunk from gold paper and adhere it to the back of the tree. Add a star to the top of the tree before attaching it to the inside back cover with foam adhesive.

6. Write the greeting on the inside back cover with a silver marker.

DECORATE THE COVER

7. Measure and cut a ¾" x 6¼" (1.9 x 15.8 cm) white paper strip. Adhere it to the cover with the adhesive roller.

8. Cut and mat a 2" x 3½" (5.1 x 8.9 cm) lighter green rectangle to a 2¼" x 3¾" (5.7 x 9.5 cm) darker green rectangle. Adhere the matted rectangles on top of the white strip. Hand write the greeting on the matted piece with a red marker.

9. Cut a 1½" x 3¾" (3.8 x 9.5 cm) rectangle of white paper and trim to create another tree. Randomly punch holes in the tree and attach over the green mat. Add a star sticker to the top.

FINDING LARGER PAPER SHEETS

Typically, the scrapbook section of a crafts store only offers 8½" x 11" (21.6 x 27.9 cm) and 12" (30.5 cm) square sheets that you have to piece together to create an accordion-fold card. To make a longer accordion without piecing, check in the art section for larger sizes of paper.

Thank Hue

Paint chips from the hardware store provide the inspiration for this colorful card. Vertical accordion pleats form the spine and hold the trimmed paint chips that become the pages. I backed each piece with a matching color chip in order to cover the text on the back. Because the paint chips are so colorful, I opted for everything else on the card to be black or white so that the colors would pop without becoming overwhelming.

TOOLS & MATERIALS

- 7¾" x 7" (19.7 x 17.8 cm) envelope
- Adhesive roller
- Craft scissors
- Fine-point markers: black, silver
- Foam adhesive
- Hole punch
- Mini brad: black
- Paint chips: 2–3 each of 12 assorted colors (30 total)
- Paper: assorted colors, black, white
- Pencil
- Ribbon: narrow black
- Rub-ons: letters, words
- Ruler
- Stickers: heart designs, words

HOW-TO

CREATE THE CARD

1. Trace the card onto white paper (see Pattern 4, page 100) and cut it out. Accordion-fold on the crease lines.

CREATE THE PAGES

2. Trim the printed labels from the paint chips and cut the chips to measure 2" x 4¼" (5.1 x 10.8 cm). Match the paint chips, creating 12 sets. Adhere the backsides of each set together, creating tags. Reserve the remaining six paint chips.

Thank Hue

3. Punch a hole in the end of each tag. Thread a black ribbon through each hole and then knot. *Note: If your ribbon is slippery, reinforce the knot with a dab of craft glue to secure it.*

4. Embellish both sides of several tags in random patterns using rub-on letters, stickers, and handwriting.

5. Adhere three paint chips in each pleat. Beginning with the top row, attach the chip tags to the front of each pleat, the middle row to the back of the pleats, and the bottom row to the pleat fronts. Trim ribbon ends as necessary so they don't extend beyond the card's edge.

CREATE THE COVERS

6. Cut four 6¼" x 7" (15.8 x 17.8 cm) square covers from white paper. Sandwich each card end between two covers and adhere them together.

7. Cut wavy strips from black paper and attach them to the inside front and back cover. Hand write messages on black strips using a silver marker.

8. Mat two paint chips with complementary paper color. Center and adhere them to the inside front and back covers. Add messages using rub-ons and stickers.

9. Cut additional wavy black strips to decorate the front cover. Write "thanks" in several languages using a silver marker.

10. Cut the remaining four paint chips into 1" x 4½" (2.5 x 11.4 cm) rectangles. Punch a hole through one end of each paint chip and stack the rectangles together. Secure the stack with a brad. Decorate the paint chips with heart stickers and rub-ons and attach them to the cover with foam adhesive.

IN OTHER WORDS . . .

- Thanks . . . You Add So Much Color to My Life
- You Color My World
- You Turn Black and White . . . into Glorious Color!

A Handful of Thanks

I'm always sending thank-you notes and helping hands offer the perfect embellishment to convey this sentiment. Try cutting the hands out of different shades of creams, tans, and browns for a very "hand-some" option. The hands are attached randomly to the front of all the pleats, creating a sea of hands that wave to you as the card sits on display. The inside greeting reads "for lending a hand."

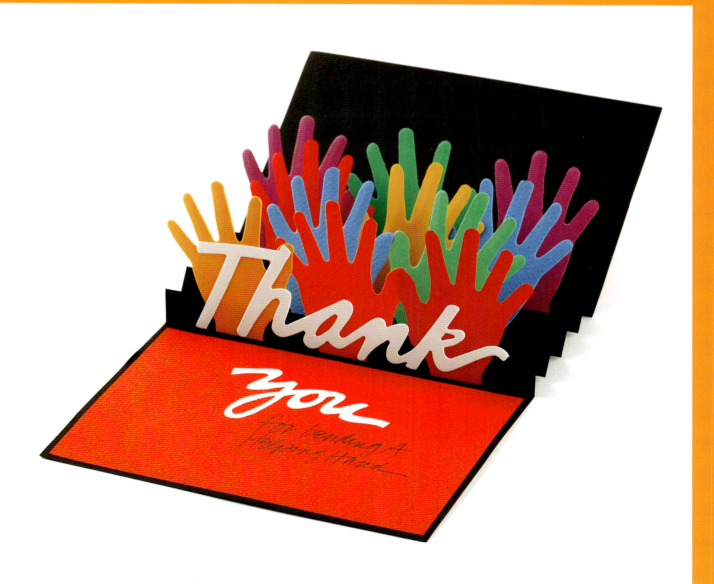

A Handful of Thanks

TOOLS & MATERIALS

- A6 envelope
- Adhesive roller
- Craft scissors
- Die cuts: hands in assorted bright colors (11), white "thank you"
- Paper: black, red
- Pencil
- Sticker: white "thanks"

HOW-TO

CREATE THE CARD

1. Trace the card onto black paper (see Pattern 4, page 100) and cut it out. Accordion-fold on the crease lines.

EMBELLISH THE INTERIOR

2. Randomly attach the hand die cuts to the front of each pleat, sometimes using two hands, other times three hands. *Note: When attaching the hands be sure to check the fingers so they don't show when the card is closed.*

3. Attach the "thank" portion of the die cut across the bottom of the first row of hands. *Note: You can also use stickers or rubber stamps.*

4. Cover the bottom of the card with red paper, leaving a ⅛" (0.3 cm) black border. Center and adhere the remaining "you" die cut on top of the red mat.

EMBELLISH THE COVER

5. Decorate the cover with a red mat, leaving a ⅛" (0.3 cm) border all around. Layer 1⅝" x 3" (4.1 x 7.6 cm) rectangle on top and add a "thanks" sticker.

IN OTHER WORDS . . .

- You Are . . . Hands Down, the Best
- You're So Handy
- Just Waving Hi! (or Good-bye)

Star Studded

Stars stuck to an accordion-folded strip appear to be floating and dancing on the tabletop in this stellar card. Because many people have white or beige walls, I decided to create the base of the card from red in order to help it really stand out when on display.

Tinkle tinkle
little bell
I hope your
holidays
are swell

TOOLS & MATERIALS

- A7 envelope
- Adhesive roller
- Cellophane tape
- Craft scissors
- Die cuts: various-sized green, red, and ivory stars (12 total)
- Embroidery floss: green
- Jingle bell: ⅜" (1.9 cm) red
- Paper: green, red
- Pencil
- Stickers: tiny heart (4)

HOW-TO

CREATE THE CARD

1. Trace the card onto red paper (see Pattern 18A, page 111) and cut it out. Accordion-fold on the crease lines. *Note: You can make the card without using the pattern by folding a long strip of paper into eight equal sections and punch a circle or square out of the center of each mountain fold.*

2. Trace the strip onto red paper (see Pattern 18B, page 111) and cut it out. Accordion-fold on the crease lines.

Star Studded

3. Push the flared ends of the red strip through the holes in the mountain folds of the card. *Note: The folds are opposite each other; each mountain fold on the card aligns with a valley fold in the strip.*

EMBELLISH THE CARD

4. Attach different sizes of ivory stars to the red strip in random order with the adhesive roller, being careful to keep each star even with the bottom of the card or higher. Fasten star collars to each ivory star. Add heart stickers to some ivory stars.

5. Decorate the middle star with a green star. Thread a 4" (10.2 cm) length of embroidery floss through a jingle bell and knot the ends. Hang the bell from the star's tip and secure the floss in place with a small piece of cellophane tape on the back.

6. Decorate the first and last section of the card with double green mats to hold a greeting and more stars.

IN OTHER WORDS . . .

- Have a Stellar Holiday
- Have a Bright & Shining Holiday
- Here's to a Star-Studded Holiday

Kiss the Old Year Good-Bye

An accordion-fold card with a square window cut out of each panel can be the format for any themed card. This becomes a Christmas card with the addition of the pairs of holiday die cuts that appear to float in the window openings. On my very first card, I wrote my greeting directly on the card below each window. If you aren't comfortable with your handwriting, print the text on red or green paper using a computer and printer. Trim the text into rectangles and fasten one to each panel. But remember, your friends know you by those things unique to you—your hair, your eyes, and yes, your handwriting.

Kiss the Old Year Good-Bye

TOOLS & MATERIALS

- A7 envelope
- Adhesive roller
- Craft knife
- Craft scissors
- Die cuts: angel, mistletoe, ornament, reindeer, tree (2 each)
- Fine-point marker: black
- Paper: cream
- Pencil

HOW-TO

CREATE THE CARD

1. Trace the card onto cream paper (see Pattern 16, page 110) and cut it out. Using a craft knife, cut out the windows and accordion-fold on the crease lines.

EMBELLISH THE CARD

2. Align each pair of die cuts and adhere them together, sandwiching parts of the window edges between them.

3. Hand write a greeting under each window opening with a black marker, if desired. Add details and facial features as desired to the die cuts.

ALTERNATIVES TO DIE CUTS

You don't have to use die cut designs to create the *Kiss the Old Year Good-Bye* card. Try rubber-stamping images or trace over old Christmas cards on vellum to make patterns and then cut your own designs by hand.

Heartfelt Thanks

This project combines an accordion-folded piece within a larger accordion and lots of dangling elements for a greeting that's sure to impress. When you send a thank-you note like this, people are likely to thank you for thanking them with such a special card.

Heartfelt Thanks

TOOLS & MATERIALS

- A7 envelope
- Adhesive roller
- Cellophane tape
- Craft knife
- Craft scissors
- Die cuts: large hearts (7), small hearts (4)
- Fine-point markers: black, red, silver
- Paper: black, deep yellow, orange, red, white, yellow
- Pencil
- Ruler
- Stickers: large stars (4), small stars (4)
- Thread: white

HOW-TO

CREATE THE CARD

1. Trace the large accordion card onto yellow paper and small accordion piece onto deep yellow paper (see Patterns 11A, 11B, page 106) and cut them out.

2. Accordion-fold on all the creases of both pieces. Cut slits on the top and bottom of the interior piece as marked on the pattern. Cut and score pop-up tabs on each mountain fold marked on the pattern using a craft knife. Line each pop-up tab with orange paper and secure with the adhesive roller.

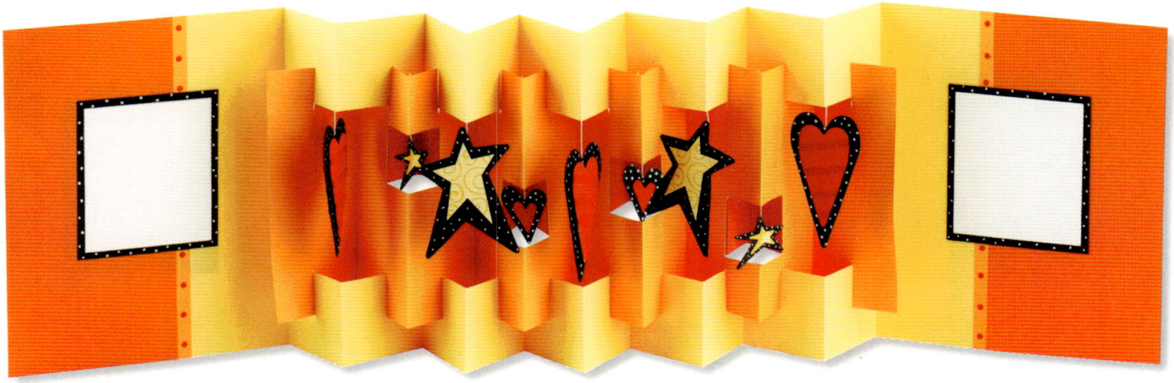

3. Hold the interior piece closed, with the first and last folds as valley folds (Fig. 1). Using the top and bottom slits, place the entire folded piece inside the opening of the larger accordion card on the left edge (Fig. 2). Hold both of the accordion pieces with your left hand and pull the right end of the interior card with your right hand, sliding it down the entire opening in the larger card and seating the interior accordion inside the larger one (Fig. 3). Adjust folds as necessary.

EMBELLISH THE INTERIOR

4. Mat seven large heart die cuts, four small heart die cuts, four large star stickers, and four small star stickers on black paper. Trim the black paper slightly larger than the heart and star shapes and dot them with a silver marker. Reserve one large heart for the card cover.

5. Pair matted stars and hearts and sandwich white thread between each set to create dangling hearts and stars. Tape the hanging embellishments behind the mountain folds on both accordion pieces so the hearts and stars hang into the cutout openings of the two pieces. Trim any thread that shows above the card top.

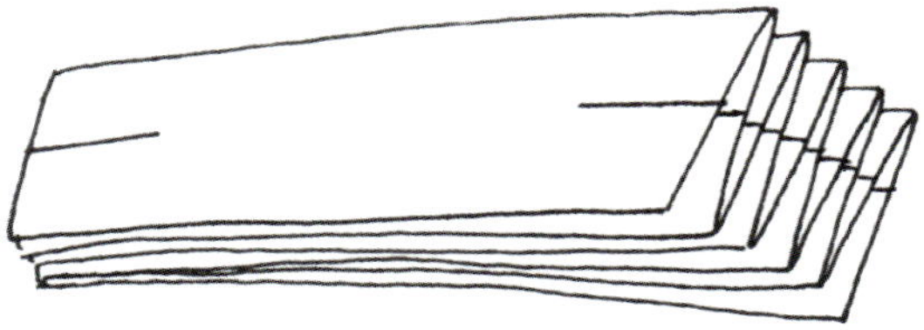

Fig. 1

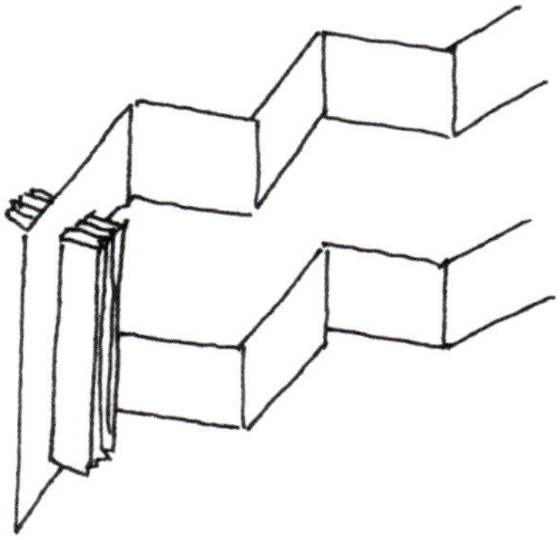

Fig. 2

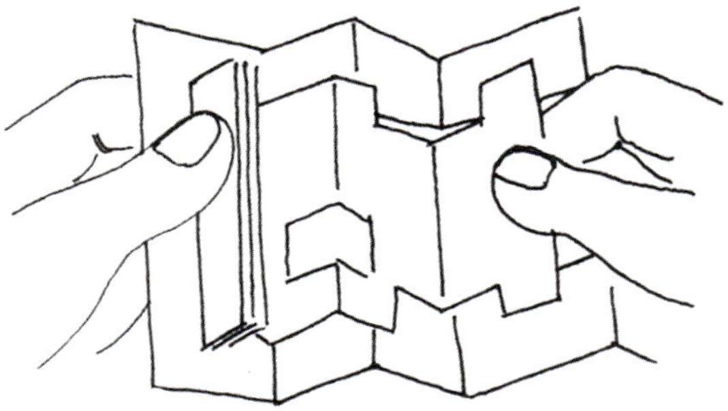

Fig. 3

Heartfelt Thanks

6. Add 3¼" (8.2 cm) orange panels to the inside front and back covers. Adhere a deep yellow paper strip over the seam and secure it with the adhesive roller. Decorate the strip with tiny red dots using a red marker.

7. Decorate the inside front and back covers with white squares matted in black and dotted with a silver marker. *Note: These areas are perfect for adding personal messages and because they are added later, you can redo them if you mess up your handwriting before attaching them to the card.*

DECORATE THE COVER

8. Decorate the front cover with a white square matted in black and dotted with a silver marker. Add the remaining matted heart and hand write a greeting in black before attaching it to the cover.

IN OTHER WORDS . . .

- You're a Superstar!
- A Hearty Hello . . . To a Star-Studded Friend
- To a Stellar Friend
- A Heartfelt Thanks

Flower Power

A bouquet of flowers can be used to represent a bridal bouquet on a unique card for a very special couple. Customize a handmade bouquet to replicate the colors of the wedding for a truly personal touch. The interlocking hearts hanging on the inside of the card are perfect for a heartfelt message.

Flower Power

TOOLS & MATERIALS

- 5¾" (14.6 cm) square envelope
- Adhesive roller
- Cellophane tape
- Craft scissors
- Die cuts: hearts (4)
- Foam adhesive
- Hole punch: ⅛"
- Paper: cream, white
- Paper punches: flower, heart, leaf
- Paper scraps: blues (2 shades), greens (2 shades), red (2 shades)
- Pencil
- Ruler
- Thread: white

HOW-TO

CREATE THE BOUQUET

1. Cut the rough shape of a bouquet from green paper. Punch flowers from various colors of paper and leaves from green paper. Cut and layer thin contrasting green stems on the base and add flowers and leaves, securing them with the adhesive roller. Occasionally raise a flower with foam adhesive to add dimension.

2. Complete the bouquet with a blue wrapper attached over the stems and raised with foam adhesive. Finish the wrapper with tiny circles punched from white paper for the buttons.

CREATE THE CARD

3. Cut the card from white paper (see Pattern 5A, page 101) and accordion-fold on the crease lines. Cut the card cover ¼" (0.6 cm) larger than the card from cream paper (see Pattern 5B, page 101). Cut a cream mat ½" (1.3 cm) smaller than the cover and fasten the bouquet to it with foam adhesive; center and adhere it to the cover with the adhesive roller.

EMBELLISH THE INTERIOR

4. Create hanging hearts by sandwiching thread between matching heart die cuts. Attach the hanging hearts with cellophane tape to the backside of the inside card, positioning them to hang inside the square opening.

5. Fasten the top and bottom panels of the card to the cover using adhesive roller.

6. Cut the stripe and dot embellishments out of white paper to decorate the inside of the card. Finish the inside with two hearts cut from different shades of red paper secured to the bottom panel.

IN OTHER WORDS . . .

- Congratulations
- With Sympathy
- Thinking of You

VARIATION

This is the announcement I created for my niece's first born. The photo on the cover is printed in sepia. Inside, stickers of baby shoes hang from the card to illustrate the pitter-patter of the two new feet. The greeting and birth information is printed on sheets of patterned paper before being trimmed into individual messages and fastened to the card. I assembled everything on the card except for the photo and birth information before the baby was born, knowing how little time there would be once she arrived on the Fourth of July.

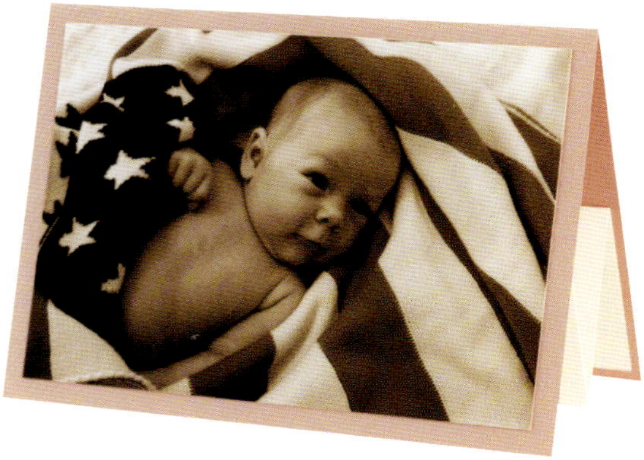

We Added Two New Feet To Our Home
The Patriotic Peanut has arrived...
Addison Brewer-Hay
6 lbs 14 ounces
20 inches long
Born July 4th, 2006 11:41 pm
Red, White and Brewed in San Francisco!!

Eat Cake

This card doubles as a mobile and is a sweet reminder of birthday wishes. Each layer of the birthday cake is decorated simply with stripes, checks, and dots, all of which can be done using a paper trimmer and circle punches. The crowning touch is the sticker candles on top. Be sure to use mirror-image stickers because both sides of the cake will show as it twirls.

Eat Cake

TOOLS & MATERIALS

- 9¼" x 6¼" (23.5 x15.8 cm) envelope
- Adhesive roller
- Craft scissors
- Hole punch
- Paper: brown (2 shades), red (2 shades), yellow
- Paper punches: ¼" (0.6 cm) circle, ⅜" (0.9 cm) circle, corner rounder
- Paper trimmer
- Ruler
- Stickers "happy birthday," mirror-image candles
- Thread: white

HOW-TO

CREATE THE CAKE TIERS

1. Measure and cut two 1¼" x 7" (3.1 x 17.8 cm), two 1" x 5" (2.5 x 12.7 cm), and two ¾" x 3" (1.9 x 7.6 cm) strips from darker brown paper. Measure and cut two 1¼" x 6" (3.1 x 15.2 cm) and two 1" x 4" (2.5 x 10.2 cm) strips from lighter brown paper. Round the corners on the top of each of the cake tiers.

2. Measure and cut two 1" x 8" (2.5 x 20.3 cm) strips from lighter red paper.

3. Decorate each cake tier with stripes, checks, and dots punched with circle punches, using contrasting brown paper. Cut two bases from matching red paper and decorate them with darker red paper dots. Adhere one base to the center of one red strip; repeat with remaining strip and base. *Note: You can save time and steps by cutting out the cake plate as one piece instead of cutting the top and base separately and then layering them together.*

ASSEMBLE THE CAKE

4. Adhere the backsides of the cake plate together, sandwiching a 22" (55.9 cm) length of thread between the strips.

5. Build the cake by matching tiers together and sandwiching the thread between each pair, allowing about ¼" between each tier and leaving the excess thread at the top for hanging the completed mobile.

6. Finish the top of the cake with mirror-image candle stickers stuck back to back.

CREATE THE TAG

7. Measure and cut a 1" x 2" (2.5 x 5.1 cm) tag shape out of yellow paper. Decorate the tag with candles on one side and a "happy birthday" sticker on the other side. Punch a hole in the end of the tag and tie it onto the thread.

ADAPTING A NEW THEME

It would be easy to change the birthday cake into a wedding or anniversary cake (or a cake for any occasion for that matter) by simply altering the theme of the stickers and the cake color.

VARIATION

A hanging holiday tree is made the same way as the Eat Cake card. Mobile cards are some of my favorite cards; I just love how they look hanging in my house. When the tree is suspended, each of the sections turns separately to create wonderful dimension. Sliding it into and out of an envelope is not very easy, so I chose an envelope with four flaps that meet in the center that I sealed with a star. You can write your greeting on a tag attached to the end of the thread or on a separate paper that sits under the tree mobile.

SINCE WE CAN'T HANG OUT THIS HOLIDAY I THOUGHT THIS WOULD BE THE NEXT BEST THING. YOU CAN HANG IT ANYWHERE... THAT'S THE BEAU-TREE OF IT. I HOPE YOUR HOLIDAYS ARE TREE MENDOUS.

Just Ducky

A baby card is the perfect place to feature little yellow ducks hanging in the openings of this three-dimensional card. Because the ducks will move with the slightest breeze, the new mom may opt to display the card in the baby's room where the wee one can enjoy the movement. The polka dot background is created with vellum stickers but could also be made with a circle punch and decorative paper. Simple black line drawing stickers overlap the polka dots and almost look hand-drawn. The windows in this card are squares, but would work just as well with circles, ovals, or rectangles.

Just Ducky

TOOLS & MATERIALS

- A7 envelope
- Adhesive roller
- Cellophane tape
- Craft knife
- Craft scissors
- Paper: white
- Paper trimmer
- Pencil
- Rub-ons: words
- Stickers: baby-themed line drawings, greetings, mirror-image ducks, vellum dots, vellum letters
- Thread: white

HOW-TO

CREATE THE CARD

1. Trace the card onto white paper (see Pattern 17, page 110) and cut it out. Using a craft knife, cut out the square window openings and then accordion-fold on the crease lines.

EMBELLISH THE CARD

2. Sandwich various lengths of white thread between mirror-image duck stickers to create the dangling ducks.

3. Attach the ducks in a random pattern to the strip above the windows on the inside of the card with cellophane tape. Trim any excess thread.

4. Place adhesive on the inside of all the card panels and fold the card into the finished X shape.

5. Decorate the card with vellum dots and baby-themed stickers. Add greetings using stickers, vellum letters, and rub-ons.

PIECING PAPER

If you have a hard time finding paper long enough for this card, simply cut the pattern in half and cut out two patterns, then piece them together, creating the same X shape.

VARIATION

The mechanics of this card are the same as the Just Ducky card, but the colors and sentiment are very different. The dangling tags in this card are stickers that can be used to complement almost any theme. Because so many of my friends are such colorful characters, this card celebrates their love of bright hues. And the embellishments couldn't be easier—simply go through your pile of paper scraps and cut thin strips of coordinating colors to decorate each of the four sides of the card. When you want bright colors to really pop, show them off with a black or white background.

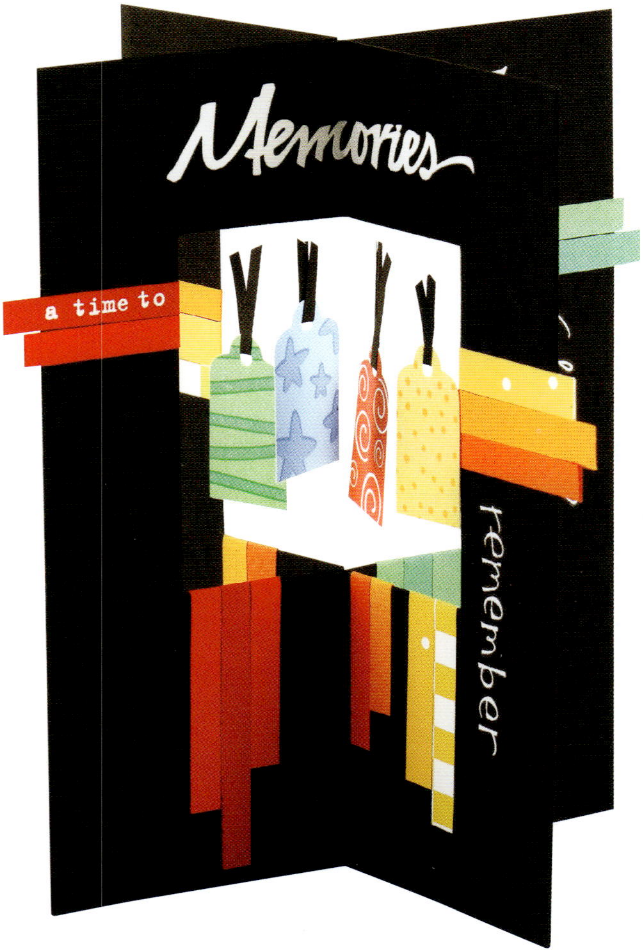

Starry, Starry Night

This is known as a star card because it creates the look of a five-pointed star when viewed from above. In addition, I opted to hang stars from each of the five sections and embellish the cover with a star to really reinforce the heavenly concept. The dimensionality of each of the five points of the star is achieved by creating the front, middle, and back sections in graduated lengths with a difference of about 1½" (3.8 cm) between each section.

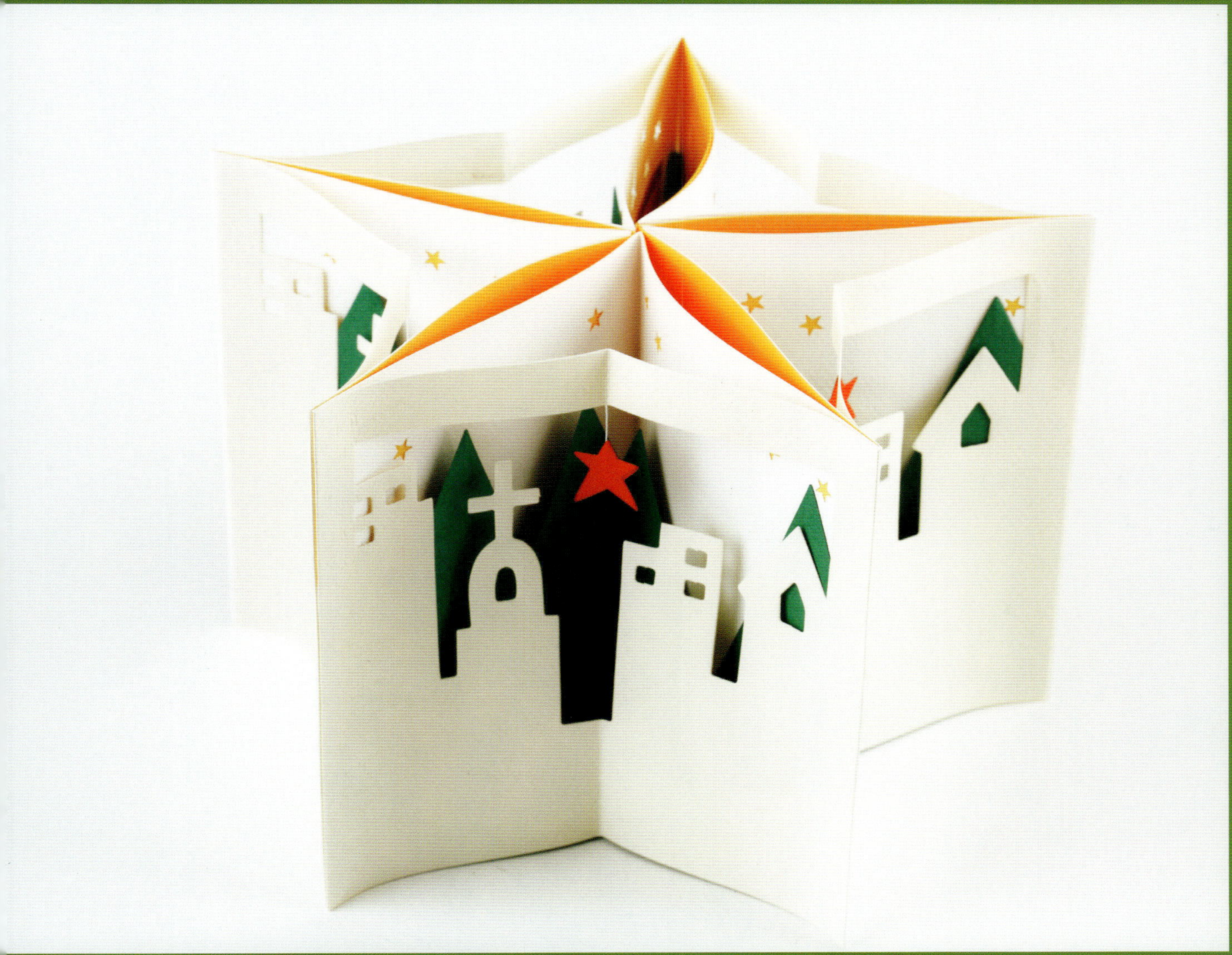

Starry, Starry Night

TOOLS & MATERIALS

- A7 envelope
- Adhesive roller
- Cellophane tape
- Craft scissors
- Foam adhesive
- Paper: dark red, green, ivory, reds (2 shades), white, yellow, yellow polka dot scrap
- Paper punches: star (2 sizes)
- Pencil
- Ribbon: narrow green
- Ruler
- Strong-hold adhesive
- Thread: white

HOW-TO

CREATE THE CARD

1. Trace five village sections onto ivory paper, five tree sections onto green paper, and five back sections onto white paper (see Patterns 15A, 15B, 15C, pages 108–109) and cut them out.

EMBELLISH THE CARD

2. Randomly punch stars across the top 2" (5.1 cm) of each white piece using the smaller star punch. Cut five strips of yellow paper and adhere them behind the punched stars in the white piece so the yellow shows through.

3. Fold all the paper pieces in half. Align the ends of one front, middle, and back section and adhere them together with the strong-hold adhesive. Repeat with the remaining sections. *Note: Cut and tape a 9" (22.9 cm) length of green ribbon between the front and back section of what will be point 1 and point 5 of the card before fastening those sections together.*

4. Punch 10 stars out of the red paper using the larger star punch. Sandwich a 2" (5.1 cm) length of white thread between two star shapes and hang them from the back of the folded front section using cellophane tape. Repeat with the remaining sections.

ASSEMBLE THE CARD

5. Fasten the completed sections together, attaching approximately ½" (1.3 cm) of the end of one section to the beginning of the next section using the strong-hold adhesive. Be sure to place the sections with ribbon at the beginning and end of the sequence. Let the adhesive set thoroughly before attempting to open the card completely.

EMBELLISH THE COVER

6. Double-mat two coordinating pieces of red paper; center and adhere them onto the cover. Cut three ½" (1.3 cm) wide strips from dark red paper and three ⅛" (0.3 cm) wide strips of green paper the same length as the smaller matted square. Layer the strips and adhere them to the matted piece using the adhesive roller. Punch a larger star from the yellow polka dot paper and attach it to the matted piece with foam adhesive. *Note: Hand write or use a computer and printer to add a greeting here.*

DISPLAY CARD

7. Pull the front of the card around to touch the back. Tie the ribbons into a bow to hold the card open.

RECIPIENT ASSEMBLY INSTRUCTIONS

8. Sometimes it's not obvious what to do with the card once the envelope is opened, so I include a small sketch of it assembled with a sentence explaining how to put the pieces together.

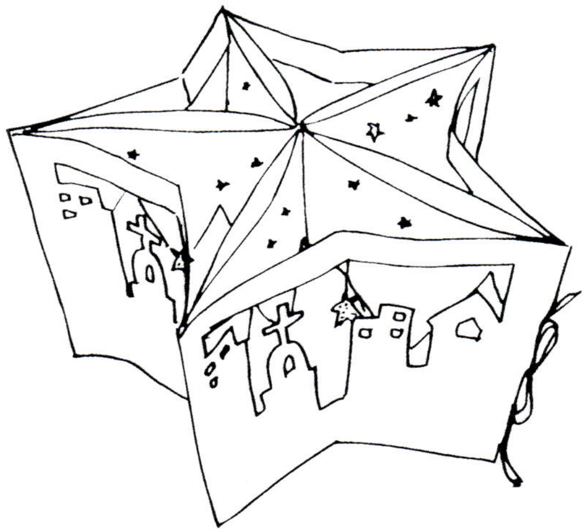

Everything is Beau-tree-ful

This three-dimensional Christmas tree, draped with a decorated spiral, is made of two interlocking triangles, one with a slit cut half way up from the bottom and the other with a slit cut half way down from the top. The tree is draped with a white spiral that is embellished with stars and a greeting. My friends tell me that they save it with their holiday decorations and display it every year.

TOOLS & MATERIALS

- A10 envelope
- Adhesive roller
- Cardstock: green
- Cellophane tape
- Craft scissors
- Fine-point markers: red, silver
- Paper: assorted colors and patterns, white (2)
- Paper punches: heart, star
- Pencil
- Stickers: mirror-image H and O letters (3 each), mirror-image tags (6)
- Thread: white

HOW-TO

CREATE THE CARD

1. Trace one of each triangle tree onto green cardstock (see Pattern 1A, page 99) and cut them out. Cut slits as marked on the patterns. *Note: The tree will stand up when the triangle slits are interlocked.*

2. Trace two spirals onto white paper (see Pattern 1B, page 99) and cut them out.

Everything is Beau-tree-ful

EMBELLISH THE TREE

3. Punch assorted hearts and stars from papers as desired. Decorate some of the shapes using red and silver markers.

4. Create dangling decorations by sandwiching a piece of white thread between each matching pair of punched shapes and mirror-image stickers and adhere the shapes together using the adhesive roller.

5. Fasten the dangling embellishments to the top of one spiral using cellophane tape. Cover the taped thread by sticking the remaining spiral on top of the first one, aligning the crosses in the center.

6. Write a greeting on the top spiral beginning in the center and following the spiral to the end.

RECIPIENT ASSEMBLY INSTRUCTIONS

7. You'll mail the tree and the spiral flat. Include a note telling the recipient to drape the embellished spiral over the assembled tree, aligning the cross in the spiral center with the top of the tree.

MAKING A SPIRAL GREETING

I find it easier to write my greeting on the spiral and then cut it into four or five segments and overlay one piece at a time on the bottom spiral.

Hearty Greetings

This unique card is made of two separate display cards rather than a single folded one. A third card acts as a stand and has double notches on its edges to support the display cards. One card is held with the half circle notches and the other is held with the rough rectangle notches. The result is that the middle support card is flanked on both sides by the bowed display cards, which is how it all stands up.

Hearty Greetings

TOOLS & MATERIALS

- 6" (15.2 cm) square envelope
- Adhesive roller
- Craft knife
- Craft scissors
- Die cuts: nested hearts
- Fine-point marker: silver
- Foam adhesive
- Paper: black, black-and-white checked, orange scraps, polka dot, red (2 shades), white, yellow (2 shades)
- Paper punch: small heart
- Paper trimmer
- Pencil
- Ribbon scraps: assorted bright colors and patterns
- Ruler
- Stickers: black-and-white striped, tiny hearts

HOW-TO

CREATE THE STAND

1. Trace the stand onto black paper (see Pattern 10, page 105) and cut it out. Cut notches in both edges using a craft knife.

2. Decorate the sides with black-and-white striped stickers. Cut a 2¾" (7 cm) square from white paper for your greeting and mat it with lighter red paper. Center and adhere the matted piece on the stand using the adhesive roller and embellish it with a small punched heart adhered with foam adhesive.

CREATE THE CARDS

3. Cut two 5½" (14 cm) square cards from black paper using a paper trimmer.

4. Cut ribbon scraps into 2½"–3" (6.4–7.6 cm) strips and attach them to the center of one card in a sunburst pattern using an adhesive roller. *Note: You can attach the entire ribbon or just the ends in the center of the starburst.*

5. Cut a 3" (7.6 cm) square from the black-and-white checked paper, mat it with the lighter red paper, and attach the piece on top of the ribbon using foam adhesive. Decorate the checked square with nested hearts die cuts in two shades of red and adhere with foam adhesive.

6. Cut a 1½" (3.2 cm) strip of polka dot paper and adhere it to the remaining card. Add a ½" (1.3 cm) band of lighter red paper that is striped with the darker red paper. Cut a lopsided heart from yellow paper and cover one side with the darker yellow paper. Mat a tiny heart sticker on a small orange square and adhere it onto the yellow heart. Attach embellished heart to the card with foam adhesive. Add silver dots around the heart with a silver marker.

RECIPIENT ASSEMBLY INSTRUCTIONS

7. An illustration of the assembled card (see below) is all that's necessary to show the recipient how to assemble the card.

MAKING NEAT NOTCHES

The shape of the notches can be whatever is easy for you to cut with a craft knife. If half circles are more challenging than you'd like, simply substitute arrowheads or any other design that is cut using straight lines. For perfectly cut notches, use a notch-cutting tool available at craft stores or online.

I Do

It's fun to showcase the typically formal photos from a wedding in a more casual way, like I did in this project featuring photos from my niece's wedding. A center card with double notches on the sides becomes a great vehicle to display a collage of wedding photos on one side and a card embellished with a silk flower in the colors of the wedding on the other side. The notches on the sides of the center card are placed so that the display cards must be bowed in order to fit into the slots that allow the assembled piece to stand.

TOOLS & MATERIALS

- A10 envelope
- Adhesive roller
- Craft knife
- Craft scissors
- Foam adhesive
- Paper: black, black-and-white checked, black-and-white floral, light orange, polka dot, pumpkin, yellow (2 shades)
- Paper punches: hearts (2 sizes), round buckle
- Paper trimmer
- Pencil
- Photos
- Ruler
- Silk flower
- Sticker: black-and-white strip

HOW-TO

CREATE THE STAND

1. Trace the stand onto lighter yellow paper (see Pattern 14, page 108) and cut it out. Cut notches in the edges using a craft knife.

2. Decorate the stand sides with sticker strips. Cut a 3" x 3½" (7.6 x 8.9 cm) rectangle from the darker yellow paper; mat with lighter yellow paper and then black-and-white checked paper. Attach the matted rectangle to the stand and embellish it with two punched red hearts. Add a large punched heart with the adhesive roller and a small heart with foam adhesive to the matted piece. Write a greeting on the darker yellow rectangle.

I Do

CREATE CARDS

3. Cut two 5½" x 8½" (14 x 21.6 cm) rectangles from yellow paper using a paper trimmer.

4. Cut three ½" (1.3 cm) strips of darker yellow paper and three ⅛" (0.3 cm) strips of light orange paper. Layer and adhere an orange strip on top of a yellow strip using the adhesive roller; repeat with the remaining strips. Adhere the layered strips on one yellow card with adhesive roller.

5. Cut one 2¼" x 3½" (5.7 x 8.9 cm) piece of pumpkin paper and one 3¾" x 5" (9.5 x 12.7 cm) piece of black-and-white floral paper. Center and adhere the pumpkin piece on the floral piece using the adhesive roller. Center the silk flower on the pumpkin piece and attach it with foam adhesive. Adhere the matted flower to the center of the embellished yellow card using the adhesive roller.

6. Adhere a collage of photos to the second card. Cut a ¼" x 8½" (0.6 x 21.6 cm) yellow paper strip and mat it with black paper. Punch a buckle from polka dot paper and thread it with the matted strip. Adhere the strip and buckle to the bottom of the card using the adhesive roller.

ASSEMBLE CARD

7. Slide the cards—one on each side—into the notches on the edges of the stand so that they bow slightly, allowing the card to stand upright.

RECIPIENT ASSEMBLY INSTRUCTIONS

8. You'll need to add instructions to tell the recipient to slide the cards—one on each side—into the notches in the stand so that they bow slightly, allowing the card to stand upright.

RECYCLING GREETING CARDS

Recycle your favorite greeting cards by using them as patterned paper in a new creation. The black-and-white floral print on this card is actually a recycled thank-you card. I just covered the greeting with pumpkin-colored paper and a silk flower.

Birthdays are a Gift

The cards that I most often make celebrate birthdays. It's a challenge to invent a unique way to say Happy Birthday each year. This card is a diorama and its dimensionality is achieved by holding the graduated layers together with colored brads. The front layer is the shortest, the back is the longest, and the middle is in between. When the holes in each corner are aligned and a brad is attached through each hole, the front remains flat and the middle and back layers create successively longer arcs that allow the card to stand.

Birthdays are a Gift

TOOLS & MATERIALS

- A10 envelope
- Adhesive roller
- Cellophane tape
- Circle punch: ⅞" (2.2 cm)
- Craft knife
- Craft scissors
- Fine-point marker: black
- Foam adhesive
- Hole punch
- Mini brads: yellow (4)
- Paper: assorted blues, black, gray (2 shades), orange, red, white, yellow
- Paper trimmer
- Pencil
- Ruler
- Stickers: balloon (8), mirror-image candles (8)

HOW-TO

CREATE THE FRAME

1. Trace the frame onto the darker gray paper (see Pattern 2, page 99) and cut it out. Using a craft knife, cut out the rectangular window. Punch circles from the lighter gray paper using the circle punch and attach them to the front layer to create a polka dot pattern using the adhesive roller.

2. Embellish the frame with candle stickers. *Note: The candles that protrude into the frame's window should be backed with mirror-image candle stickers.*

CREATE THE SECOND LAYER

3. Cut a 1½" x 7¾" (3.2 x 19.7 cm) strip from the black paper. Embellish it with gifts cut from assorted colors of paper. Attach lids to the boxes with foam adhesive. Adhere the gifts to the black strip using the adhesive roller and then reinforce them with cellophane tape on the back of the strip.

CREATE THE THIRD LAYER

4. Cut a 5¾" x 8¾" (14.6 x 22.2 cm) rectangle from the white paper and embellish it with balloon stickers. *Note: Some of the balloons are raised with foam adhesive.* Add balloon strings with a black marker.

ASSEMBLE THE CARD

5. Punch holes in all four corners of the card's frame and third layer and in the bottom corners of the middle layer using a hole punch.

6. Stack the layers and align the holes on the left side of the card; insert the brads, flattening the prongs on the back of the white card. Repeat with the remaining brads on the right side of the card so the middle and back layers bow out, allowing the card to stand.

STORE OR MAIL THE CARD

7. Remove the brads from one side and re-attach to the top layer so the card lies flat before inserting in the envelope.

RECIPIENT ASSEMBLY INSTRUCTIONS

8. Include a note in the envelope with the card telling the recipient to thread the brads through the holes on the side and re-attach so that the card bows out and stands up.

VARIATION

One of my favorite things about this diorama card is its diversity, and it is easy to make for different occasions. Without changing the colors or the embellishments, this card could work well for a wedding or engagement or as a valentine. While the frame opening for this project is a rectangle, I have created dioramas with many different types of openings such as a circle, oval, and even a window with multiple panes.

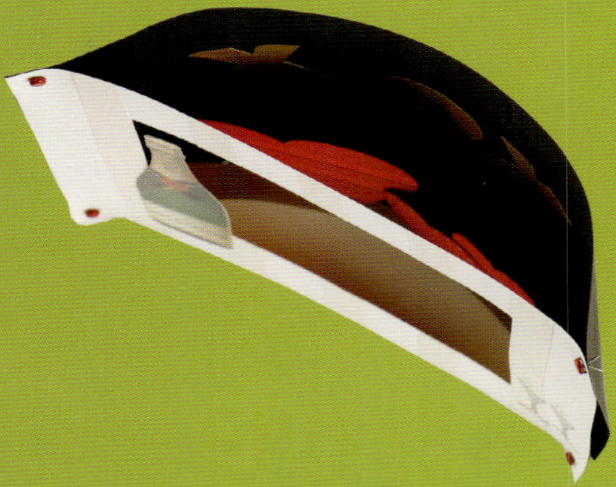

3-D Tree-t

This dimensional tree is created by pulling up the four points of a pointed cross. The sides of the tree are held in place by sliding colored bands with progressively larger squares cut out of their centers. The tree is topped with two stars, one of which dangles gifts. I had to reverse fold two of the cross's points in order to fit this card into an envelope.

3-D Tree-t

TOOLS & MATERIALS

- 7⅞" x 8" (20 x 20.3 cm) envelope
- Adhesive roller
- Cellophane tape
- Craft scissors
- Heavyweight paper: 20" (50.8 cm) square white (2)
- Paper: green, green polka dot, metallic gold, red, red polka dot
- Pencil
- Stickers: mirror-image gifts (10)
- Thread: white

HOW-TO

CREATE CARD BASE

1. Trace two tree pieces onto white heavyweight paper (see Pattern 6A, page 102) and cut them out. Overlap the midsection of each piece to form a pointed cross and fasten the square sections together with the adhesive roller.

2. Trace the bands and stars onto assorted colored and patterned papers (see Patterns 6B, 6C, 6D, 6E, 6F, pages 102-103) and cut them out. *Note: Cut two of the large stars from patterned papers.*

MAKE GIFTS

3. Sandwich white thread between mirror-image gift stickers to create the hanging gifts. Tape the ends of the thread to the wrong side of one star and then adhere the two stars together using the adhesive roller, sandwiching the taped thread in the middle.

RECIPIENT ASSEMBLY INSTRUCTIONS

4. Take a digital photograph of the assembled card and print it out in a small size. Tuck the photo in with the card pieces so that the recipient can easily see how it fits together.

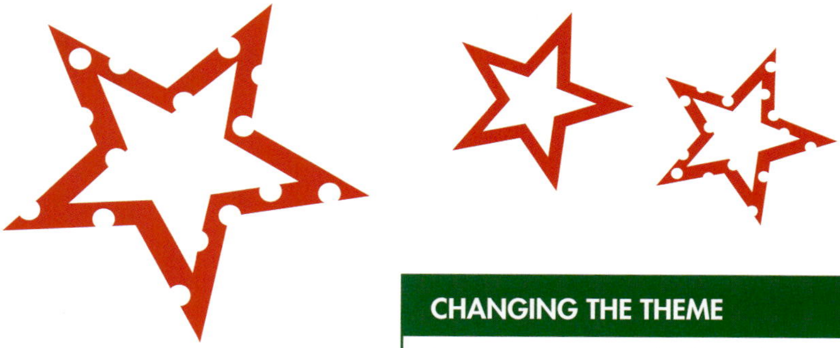

CHANGING THE THEME

I chose to hang gifts from the star but you can pick other embellishments to fit your own holiday theme such as small stars, jingle bells, or stockings, or use letters to spell "Joy." It's also possible to change the theme to fit other occasions. A family tree might be decorated with leaf stickers.

An Open and Shut Case

I discovered that my friends really enjoy getting a card that they can play with, so I started making animated cards like this one. The movement is created by holding the skewer between your hands and rotating the card back and forth. This card needs a little direction on what the card recipient should do with it, so I simply hand wrote the directions on the card holder.

Twist back & forth to see the box open & close
Enjoy
HAPPY BIRTHDAY

TOOLS & MATERIALS

- #10 envelope
- Adhesive roller
- Bamboo skewer
- Circle punches: various sizes (3–4)
- Craft knife
- Craft scissors
- Fine-point markers: black, silver
- Foam adhesive
- Garden shears
- Hole punch
- Paper: black, cream, red (2 shades), various colored scraps
- Pencil
- Ruler
- Sticker: "happy birthday"

HOW-TO

CREATE THE CARD HOLDER

1. Trace the card holder onto the lighter red paper (see Pattern 20, page 113) and cut it out. Using a craft knife, cut the slits that are marked on the pattern. Make tiny holes at the slit ends with a hole punch to prevent tearing.

EMBELLISH THE CARD HOLDER

2. Punch three different-sized circles from darker red paper using circle punches. Embellish the card with circles and the "happy birthday" sticker. Adhere the largest circle on the card so the circle overlaps the edge using the adhesive roller; trim the excess paper. Write the directions on the largest circle using a silver marker.

An Open and Shut Case

CREATE THE CARD

3. Cut a 7¾" (19.7 cm) length of bamboo skewer using garden shears. Cut two 3" x 3½" (7.6 x 8.9 cm) cards from the cream paper. Sandwich the skewer between the cards and adhere them together using the adhesive roller.

4. Cut two freehand gift boxes and lids from black paper and add dots with the silver marker. Embellish both boxes and lids with red ribbons and bows cut from the lighter red paper. Attach one box bottom to one side of the card. Attach the lid to the card so that the box appears closed using foam adhesive.

5. Punch various-sized circles from assorted colored papers for balloons using the circle punches. Adhere the second gift box, lid, and balloons to the backside of the card so the lid is open, allowing the balloons to float out of the box. Draw the balloon strings with a black marker.

6. Slide the decorated skewer through the slits on the card holder.

ANIMATION IDEAS

You don't have to be an artist to make a card like this. Some simple animation themes include:

- Something that grows and shrinks like a dot that becomes a larger circle.
- Something that opens and closes like a gift box.
- Something that moves up and down like the arms and legs of a stick figure doing jumping jacks.

Joyful

This interactive card has a hidden message that's revealed when the slider is moved to the right. Once you've used the pattern to re-create this card, you may enjoy experimenting with your own cards in different sizes with a different number of letters. You can expand or reduce the number of letters to be framed by adding or eliminating sections of the slider frame pattern.

Joyful

TOOLS & MATERIALS

- #10 envelope
- Adhesive roller
- Cardstock: cream, green (2 shades), red
- Circle punch: ½" (1.3 cm), 1½" (3.8 cm), 1¾" (4.4 cm)
- Craft knife
- Craft scissors
- Fine-point marker: red
- Foam adhesive
- Hole punch
- Paper: red
- Paper trimmer
- Pencil
- Stickers: arrow, bows, holiday greeting

HOW-TO

CREATE THE CARD

1. Trace the card onto cream cardstock (see Pattern 13A, page 107) and cut it out. Cut the slit with a craft knife and fold on the crease lines.

EMBELLISH THE CARD

2. Cover both sides of the top third of the card with lighter green cardstock. Cut ¾" x 3⅝" (1.9 x 9.2 cm) darker green strips and adhere them onto the outside cover using the adhesive roller.

3. Cut a 2" x 5" (5.1 x 12.7 cm) rectangle from red cardstock and mat it with cream cardstock. Punch ½" (1.3 cm) circles from red paper and adhere them to the matted rectangle. Add the holiday greeting sticker and attach the decorated greeting to the center of the cover with foam adhesive.

4. Cut a ¾" x 8½" (1.9 x 21.6 cm) strip from darker green cardstock. Center and adhere it to the inside cover with the adhesive roller.

MAKE THE JINGLE BELLS

5. Punch a 1½" (3.8 cm) and a 1¾" (4.4 cm) circle from cream cardstock. Punch two holes in the bottom half of each circle using the hole punch and then cut a slightly curved V from the holes to the bottom of the circle.

6. Overlap the jingle bells and attach them to the inside cover, adhering the large bell with the adhesive roller and raising the smaller one with foam adhesive. Add sticker bows to the bells.

CREATE THE SLIDER

7. Trace the slider and frame onto the red cardstock (see Patterns 13B, 13C, page 107) and cut them out. Cut the rectangle with slits out of the slider and the inner section of the frame with a craft knife. Embellish the frame with strips cut from red cardstock.

8. Attach the embellished frame to the tab portion of the slider with the adhesive roller, aligning the frame opening with the slider opening. Add the arrow sticker on the center far right end of the slider.

9. Place the slider in the card by inserting the frame portion through the slit from the backside. Add the first part of the greeting so it reads through the frame opening. Using the pattern as a guide, color in the negative space around what will become the white letters that spell "JOY" when the slider is pulled all the way to the right.

VARIATION

A sliding card is fun for many celebrations, and interactivity turns an ordinary card into an extraordinary one. This card has a slider that moves when the viewer pulls on the arrow. It becomes a frame that makes the symbols on the right suddenly turn into a Halloween message. Convert the card to a baby card by changing the colors and the message to "Peek-A-Boo."

Blow out the Candles

A card with a flip-flop feature is one of the simplest to make. It's cut from a single piece of paper with just a few slits and folds that result in an area that flips back and forth to provide a greeting or embellishment on both the front and backside of the rectangle.

Blow out the Candles

TOOLS & MATERIALS

- 5¾" (14.6 cm) square envelope
- Adhesive roller
- Craft knife
- Craft scissors
- Fine-point markers: black, silver
- Foam adhesive
- Paper: black, white, yellow
- Pencil
- Rub-ons: letters
- Stickers: balloons (5), birthday words (3–4), candles (8)

HOW-TO

CREATE THE CARD

1. Trace the card onto yellow paper (see Pattern 3, page 100) and cut it out. Using a craft knife, cut on the cut lines and then fold on the crease lines.

EMBELLISH THE CARD

2. Decorate the flip-flop feature on the front with a black square matted on white and enhanced with black dots. Embellish the black square with candle stickers, raising some with foam adhesive.

3. Add birthday word stickers around the cutout edges of the flip-flop element on the card front.

4. Decorate the back of the flip-flop with a white rectangle matted on black and enhanced with silver dots. Embellish the white rectangle with balloon stickers and draw balloon strings with a black marker. Trim the stickers wherever they overlap the edge of the white rectangle.

5. Place an additional greeting along the edge of the cutout on the back panel using rub-ons.

IN OTHER WORDS . . .

- Blow Out the Candles . . . May All Your Wishes Come True
- May All Your Wishes Come True Today . . . And All Year Long
- Celebrate! . . . It's Your Special Day

VARIATION

An animated card such as this can express good wishes for many reasons. The flipping effect on this card is created with a single accordion fold in the middle of the card with a portion of the midsection cut so that it moves freely. Because all of the cut lines are in the interior of the card, you need to cut them with a craft knife; don't worry about the lines being perfectly straight as they will be covered with a square on one side and a rectangle on the flip side.

Moving Money Magic

Giving a check, cash, or a gift certificate can seem impersonal, but not if you give it in this magical card. When you open the card in the traditional way, like a book, the money and note are on opposite sides behind the paper strips. When you close the card and open it again from the opposite side, the money and note have magically switched sides. This type of card is easy to make and fun to receive.

Moving Money Magic

TOOLS & MATERIALS

- 3¾" x 7" (9.5 x 17.8 cm) envelope
- Adhesive roller
- Craft scissors
- Fine-point marker: black
- Foam adhesive
- Paper: black, green (2 shades), red (2 shades), various colored scraps, white
- Paper punches: ½" (1.3 cm) circle, ½" (1.3 cm) square
- Ruler
- Stickers: birthday words, mirror-image candles, party blowers

HOW-TO

CREATE THE CARD

1. Cut four 3" x 6½" (7.6 x 16.5 cm) cards from the black paper and four ½" x 5" (1.3 x 12.7 cm) strips from the lighter red paper (see Pattern 12, page 106).

2. Weave the strips over and under the two black cards as shown (see Fig. 1, page 95). *Note: The 3" (7.6 cm) lengths that span the card fronts remain loose; the 1" (2.5 cm) ends that wrap around to the backsides are secured with the adhesive roller.* Cover the strips on the back with the remaining black cards.

DECORATE THE INTERIOR

3. Cut four ¼" x 3" (0.6 x 7.6 cm) darker red strips. Fasten them to the woven strips using the adhesive roller.

4. Add embellishments to the strips, avoiding the middle on the right side where the strips are spaced widely apart. On the opposite side, add mirror-image candle stickers only in the middle between the red strips. *Note: The embellishments must be two-sided because both sides will show when the card is opened and closed from opposite directions.*

5. Cut a 2⅝" x 6⅛" (6.7 x 15.5 cm) piece from white paper and embellish it with candle and party blower stickers. Write a greeting on the note with a black marker. Slip the note in one side and the money in the other side.

INCLUDE INSTRUCTIONS

When you send this card you will need to include instructions somewhere on the card so the recipient understands how to enjoy the card's secret.

EMBELLISH THE COVER

6. Punch 14 squares from white paper using the square paper punch. Attach them in a checkerboard pattern on the top and bottom of the cover using the adhesive roller.

7. Cut wobbly circles in graduated sizes from colored paper scraps. Layer and adhere the larger two layers together. Punch two ½" (1.3 cm) circles from coordinating papers and adhere them to the center of each flower using foam adhesive. Cut stems and leaves from both shades of green paper using craft scissors and attach them to the card with the adhesive roller. Adhere the assembled flowers on the stem ends.

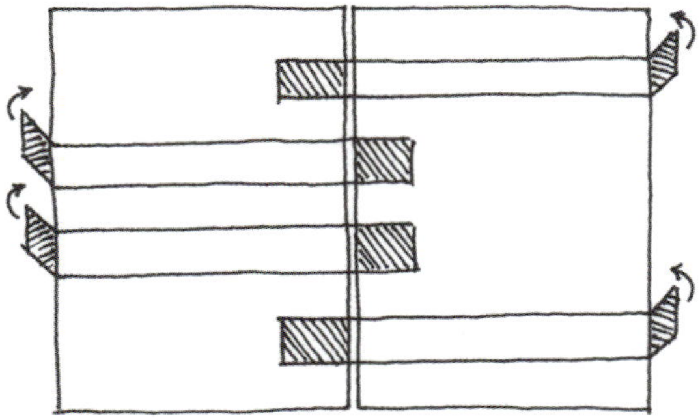

Fig. 1

VARIATIONS

A moving magic card can celebrate winter holidays, a new baby, or a special vacation. Change the dimensions of the card to allow it to hold a photo. This is a unique way to send the annual family photo with a holiday letter, or change the paper color and use baby-themed embellishments and it becomes a birth announcement. It's also a clever way to send a stack of photos showcasing your summer vacation for loved ones far away.

little one

Patterns

Pattern 1A (enlarge 200%)

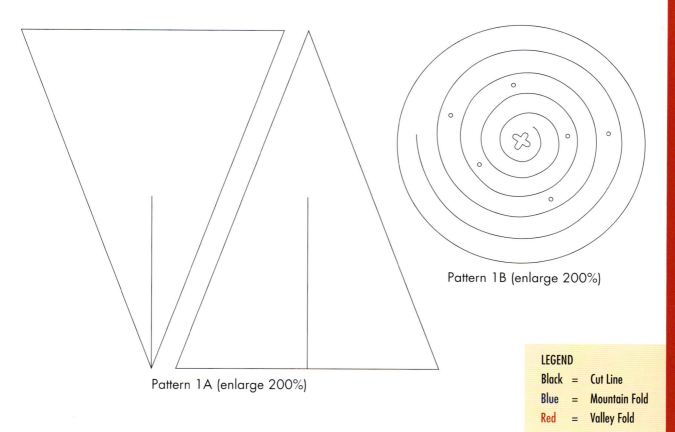

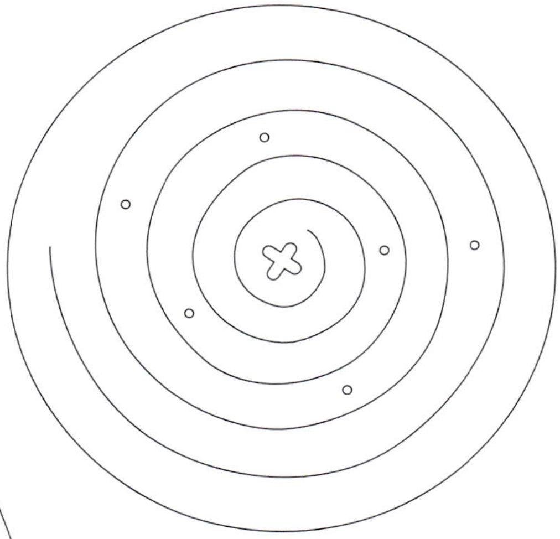

Pattern 1B (enlarge 200%)

LEGEND

Black = Cut Line

Blue = Mountain Fold

Red = Valley Fold

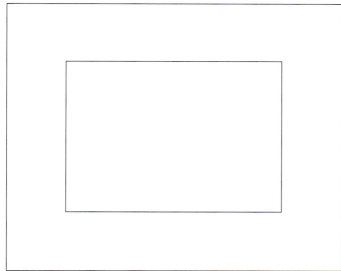

Pattern 2 (enlarge 200%)

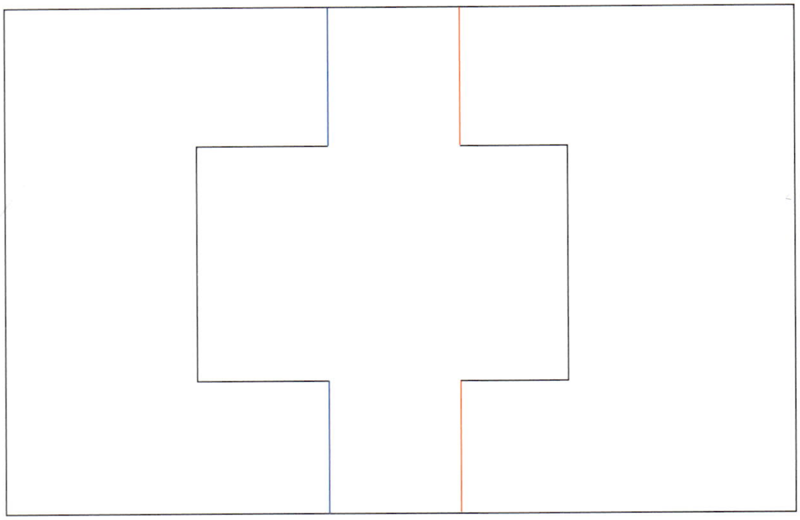

Pattern 3 (enlarge 200%)

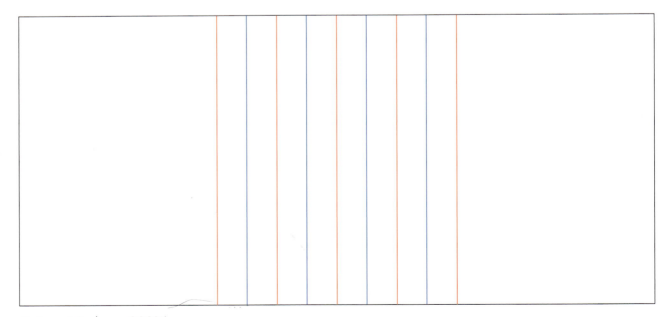

Pattern 4 (enlarge 200%)

Pattern 5A (enlarge 200%)

LEGEND
Black = Cut Line
Blue = Mountain Fold
Red = Valley Fold

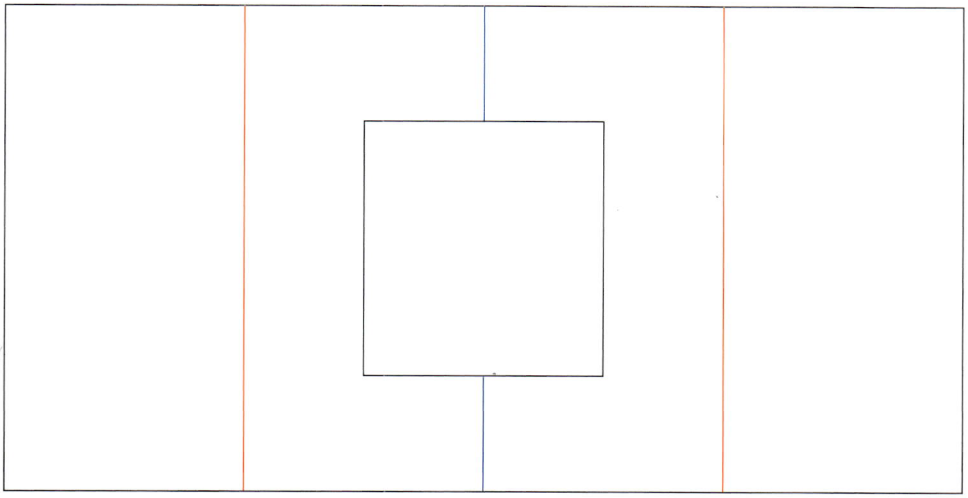

Pattern 5B (enlarge 200%)

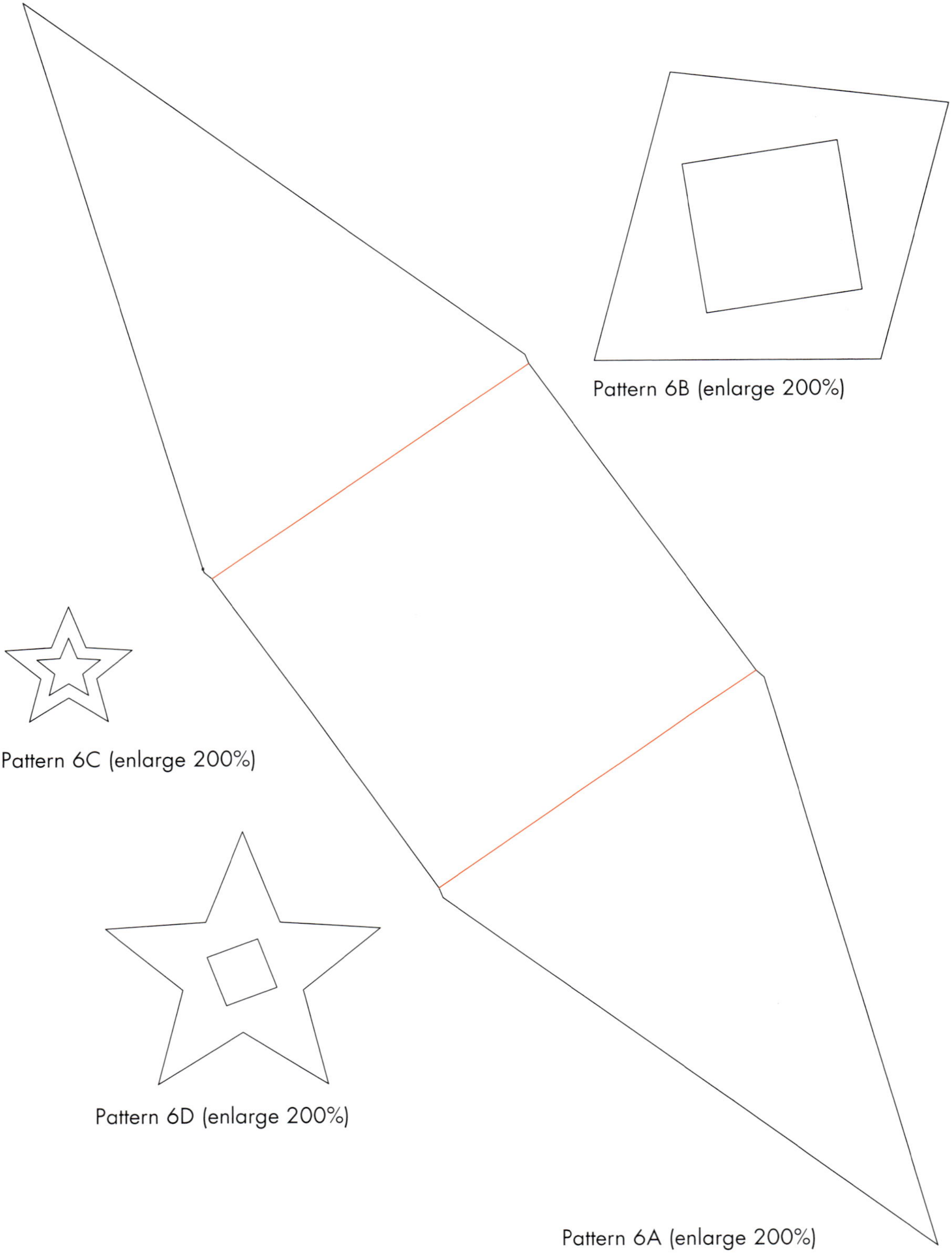

Pattern 6B (enlarge 200%)

Pattern 6C (enlarge 200%)

Pattern 6D (enlarge 200%)

Pattern 6A (enlarge 200%)

LEGEND

Black = Cut Line
Blue = Mountain Fold
Red = Valley Fold

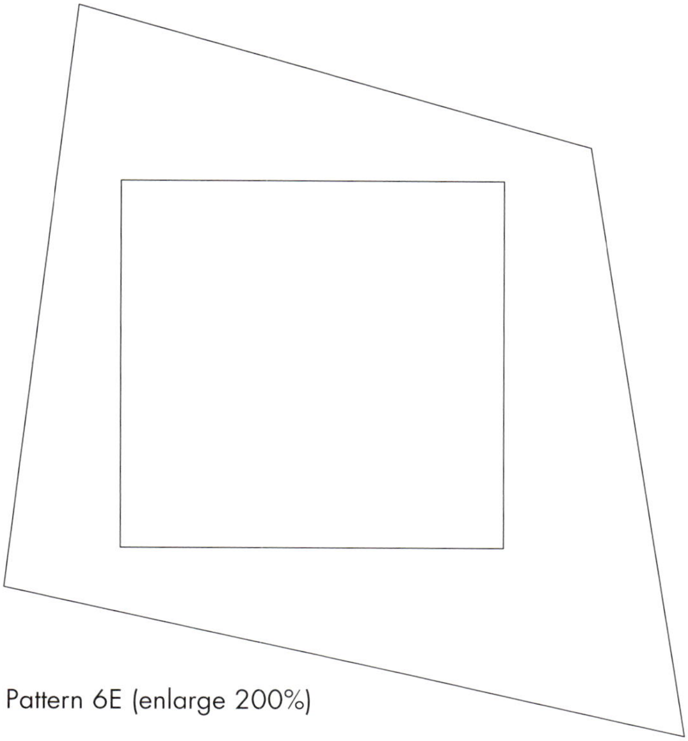

Pattern 6E (enlarge 200%)

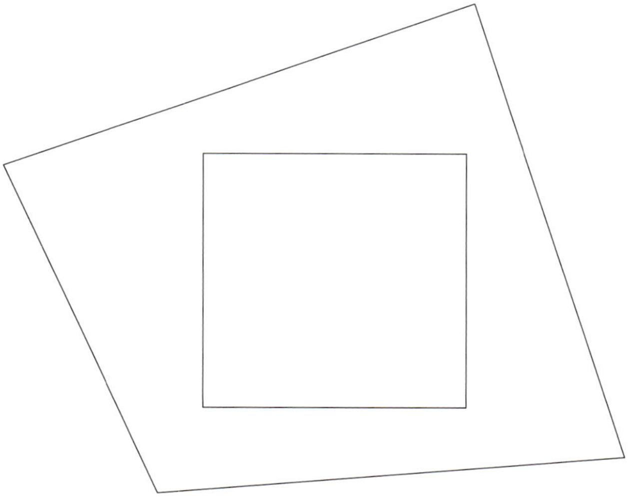

Pattern 6F (enlarge 200%)

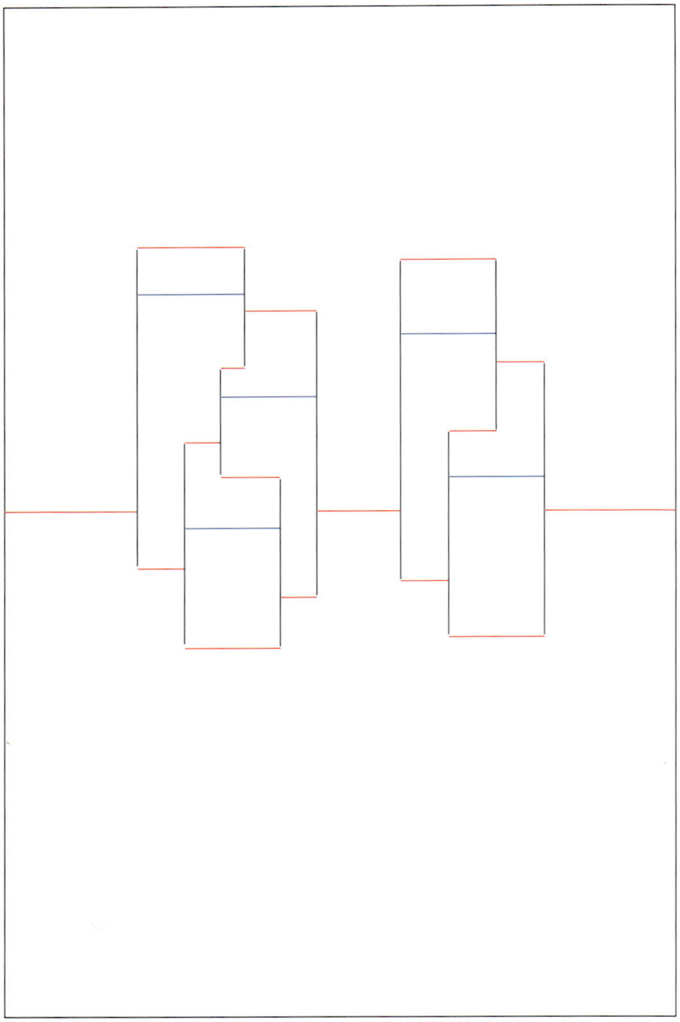

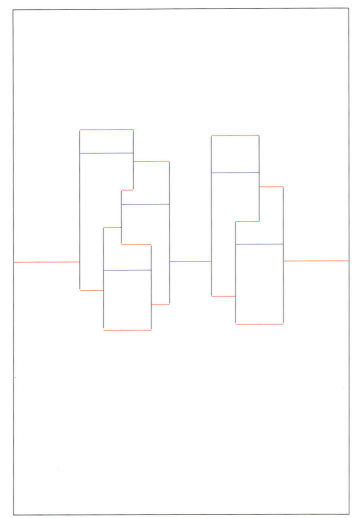

Pattern 7 (enlarge 200%)

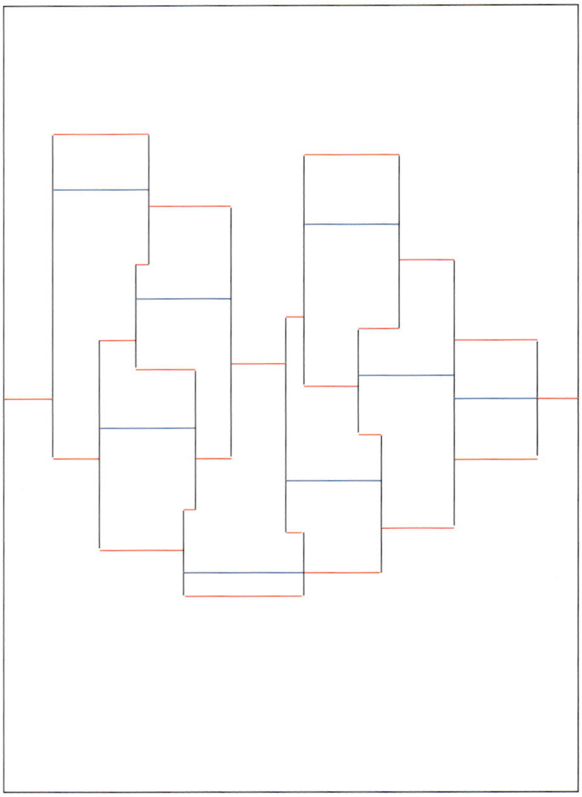

Pattern 8 (enlarge 200%)

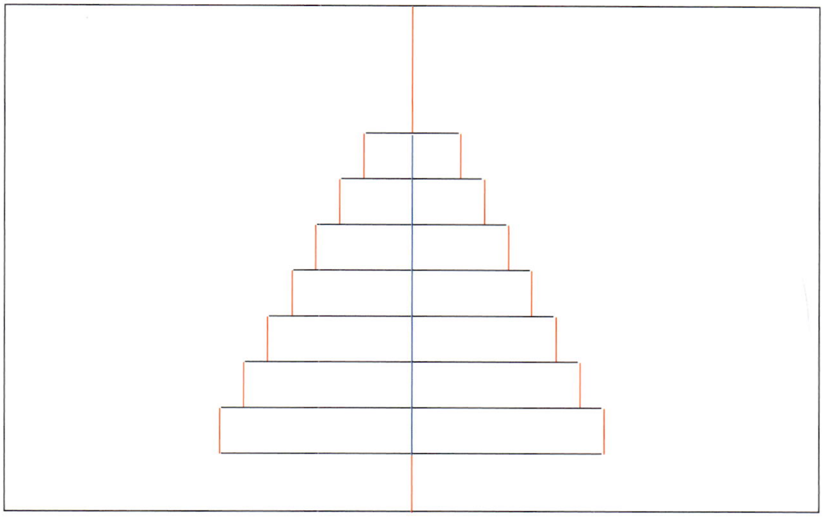

Pattern 9 (enlarge 200%)

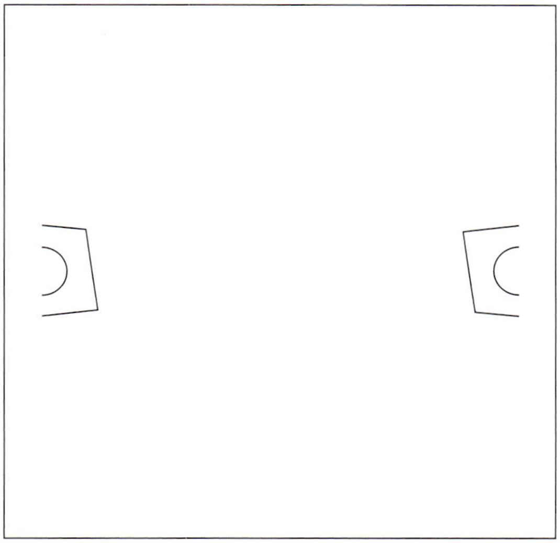

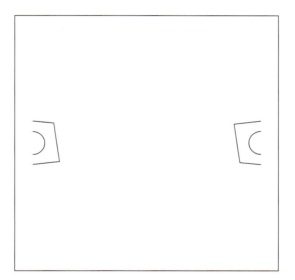

Pattern 10 (enlarge 200%)

LEGEND

Black = Cut Line

Blue = Mountain Fold

Red = Valley Fold

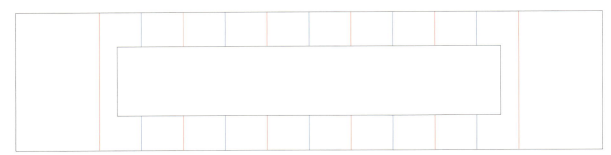

Pattern 11A (enlarge 400%)

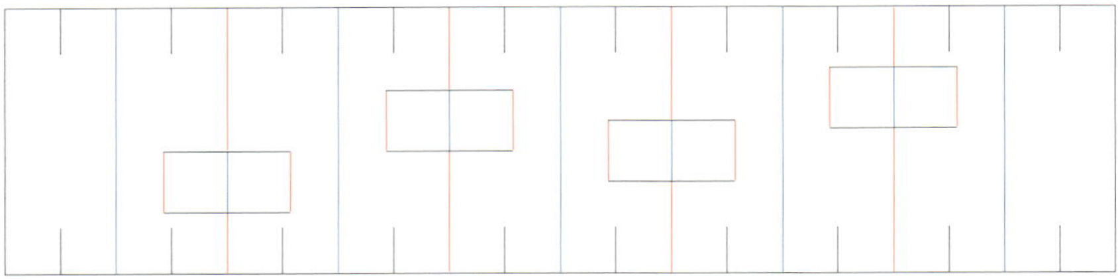

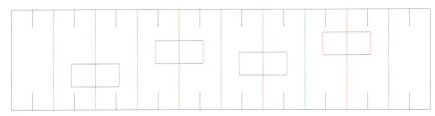

Pattern 11B (enlarge 400%)

Pattern 12 (enlarge 200%)

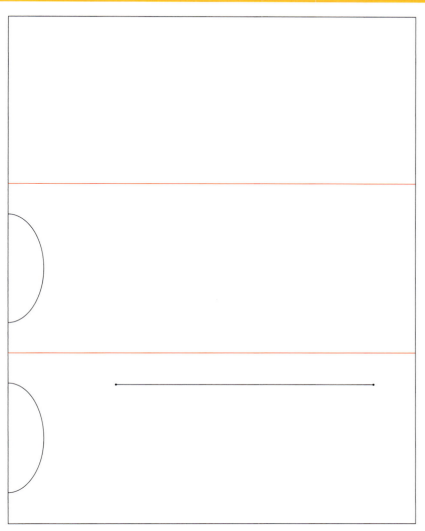

Pattern 13A (enlarge 200%)

LEGEND		
Black	=	Cut Line
Blue	=	Mountain Fold
Red	=	Valley Fold

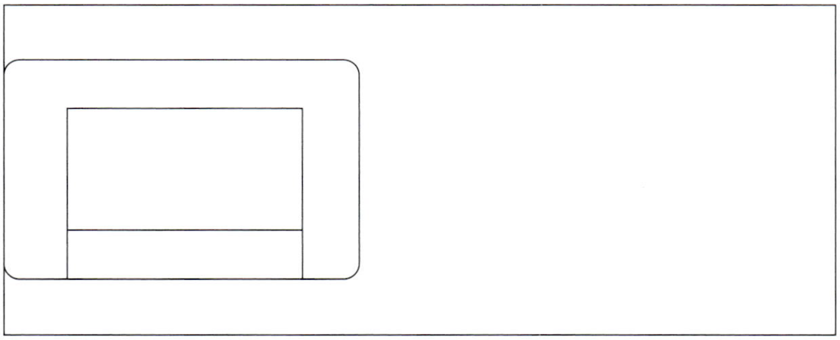

Pattern 13B (enlarge 200%)

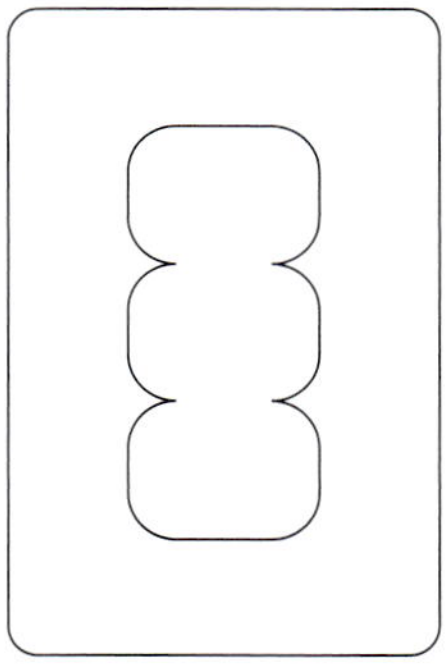

Pattern 13C (enlarge 200%)

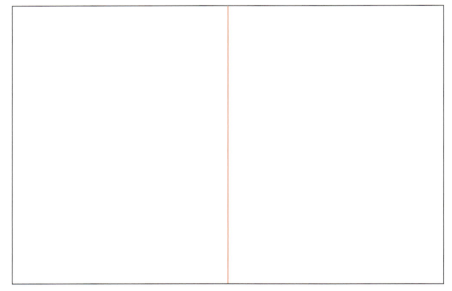

Pattern 14 (enlarge 200%)

Pattern 15A (enlarge 200%)

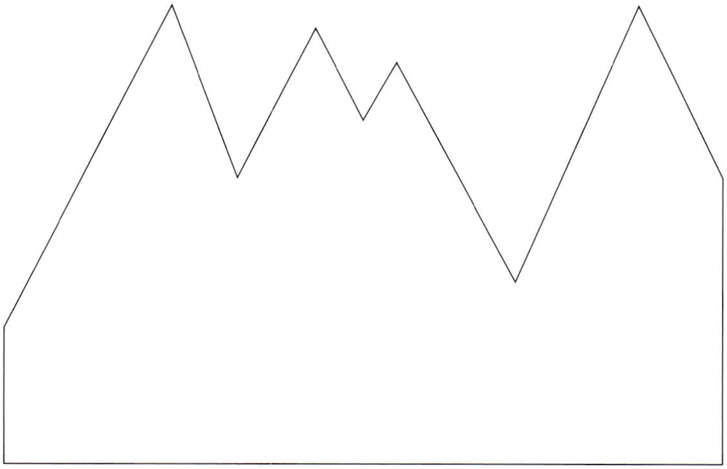

Pattern 15B (enlarge 200%)

LEGEND

Black = Cut Line

Blue = Mountain Fold

Red = Valley Fold

Pattern 15C (enlarge 200%)

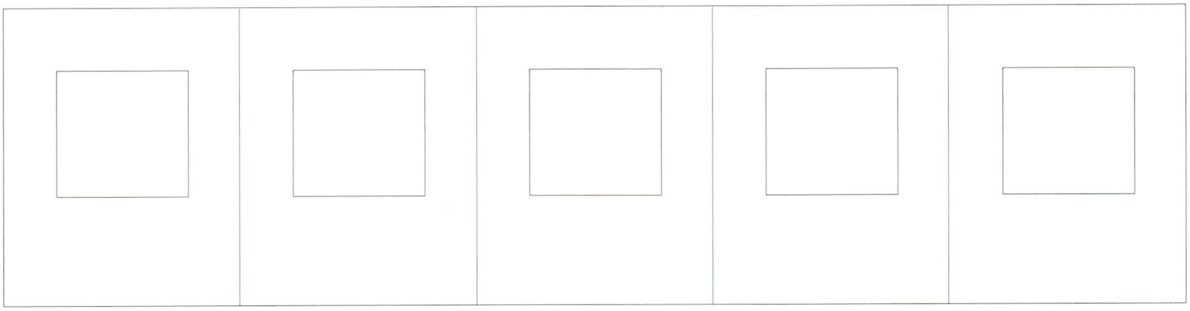

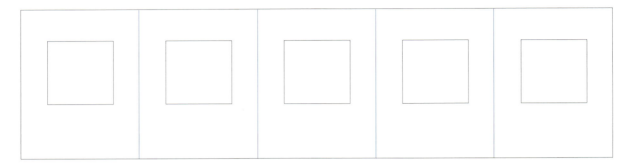

Pattern 16 (enlarge 400%)

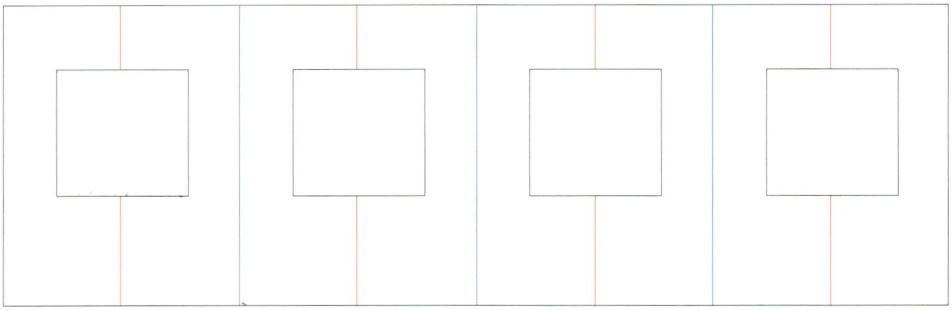

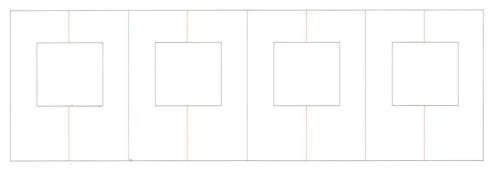

Pattern 17 (enlarge 400%)

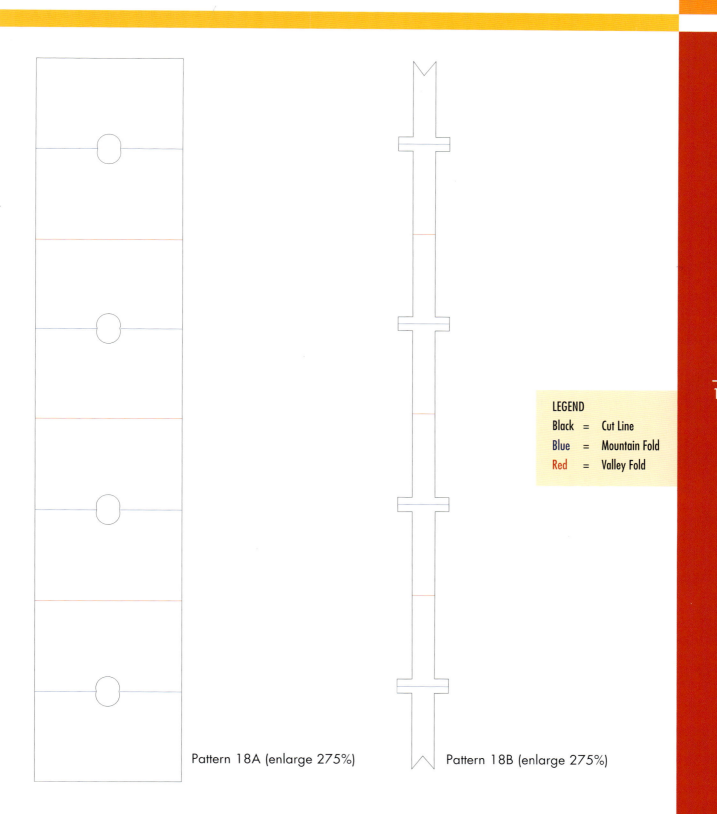

Pattern 18A (enlarge 275%)

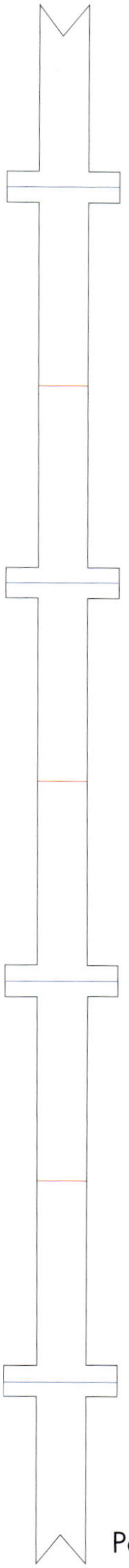
Pattern 18B (enlarge 275%)

LEGEND

Black = Cut Line

Blue = Mountain Fold

Red = Valley Fold

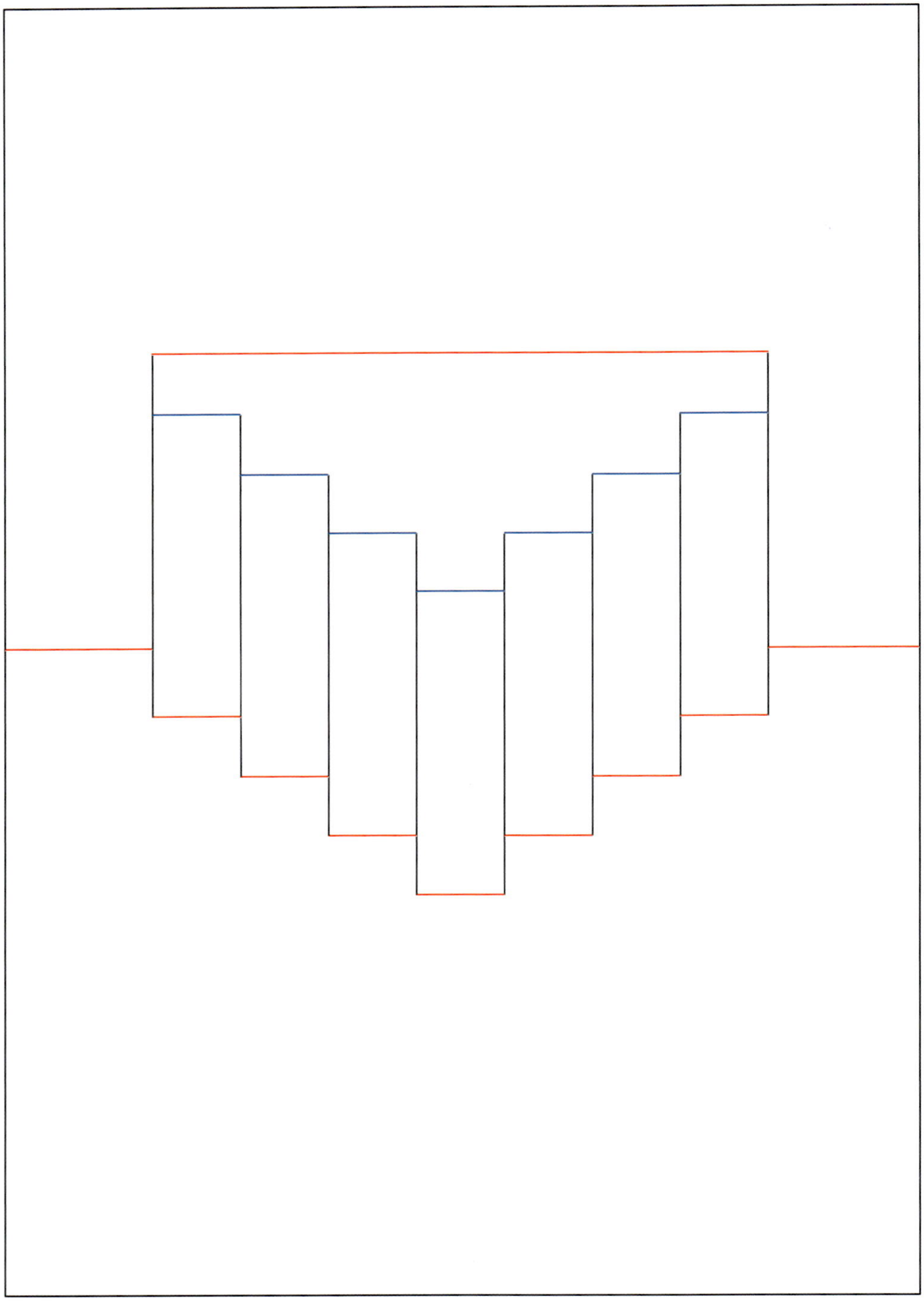

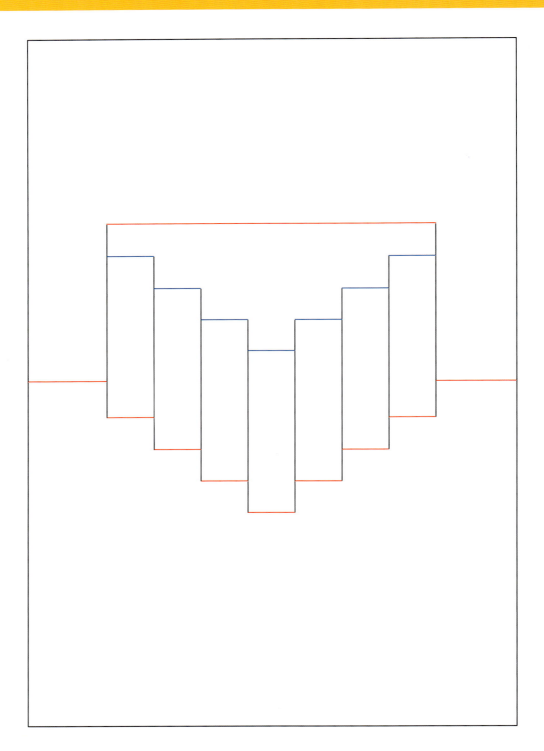

Pattern 19 (enlarge 150%)

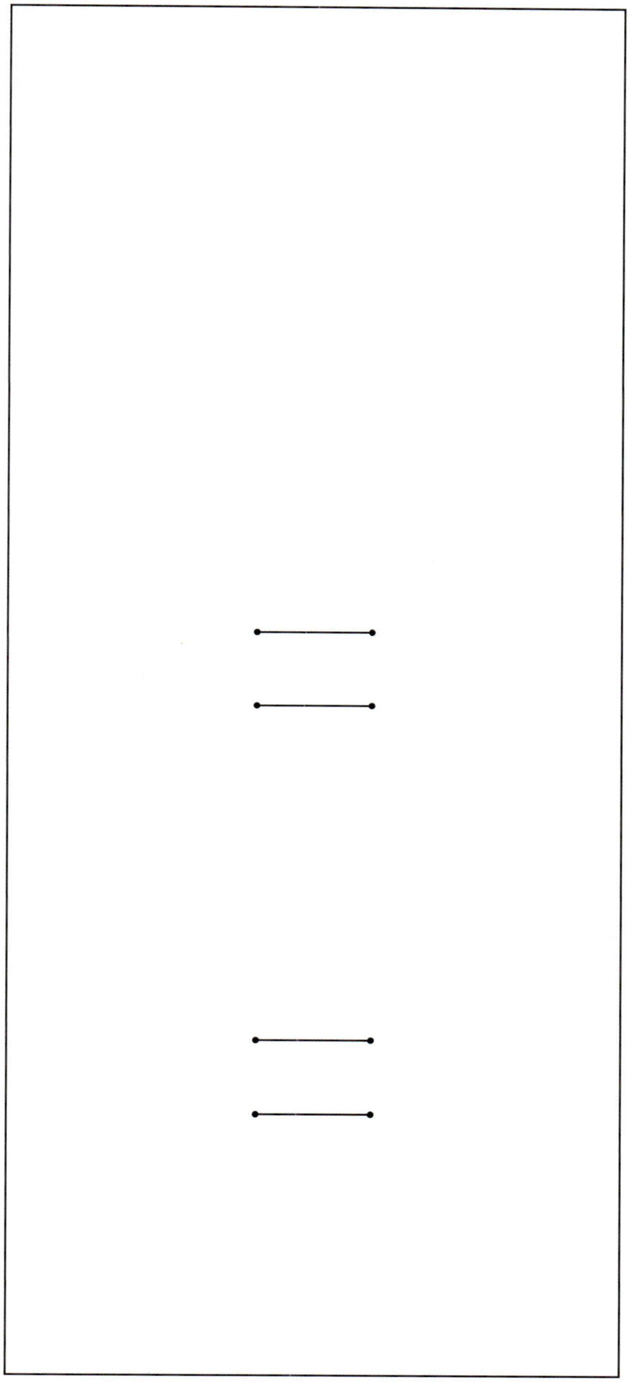

LEGEND

Black = Cut Line

Blue = Mountain Fold

Red = Valley Fold

Pattern 20 (enlarge 150%)

Envelopes

Envelope Patterns

To make an envelope, enlarge the pattern as specified on a photocopier or scan it into your computer, manipulate it using software, and print it out. Lightly trace the pattern onto paper, cut it out with craft scissors, and fold on the crease lines. Adhere the envelope edges with the adhesive roller. Once your card is complete and you're ready to mail it, seal the envelope with the adhesive roller or use a sticker.

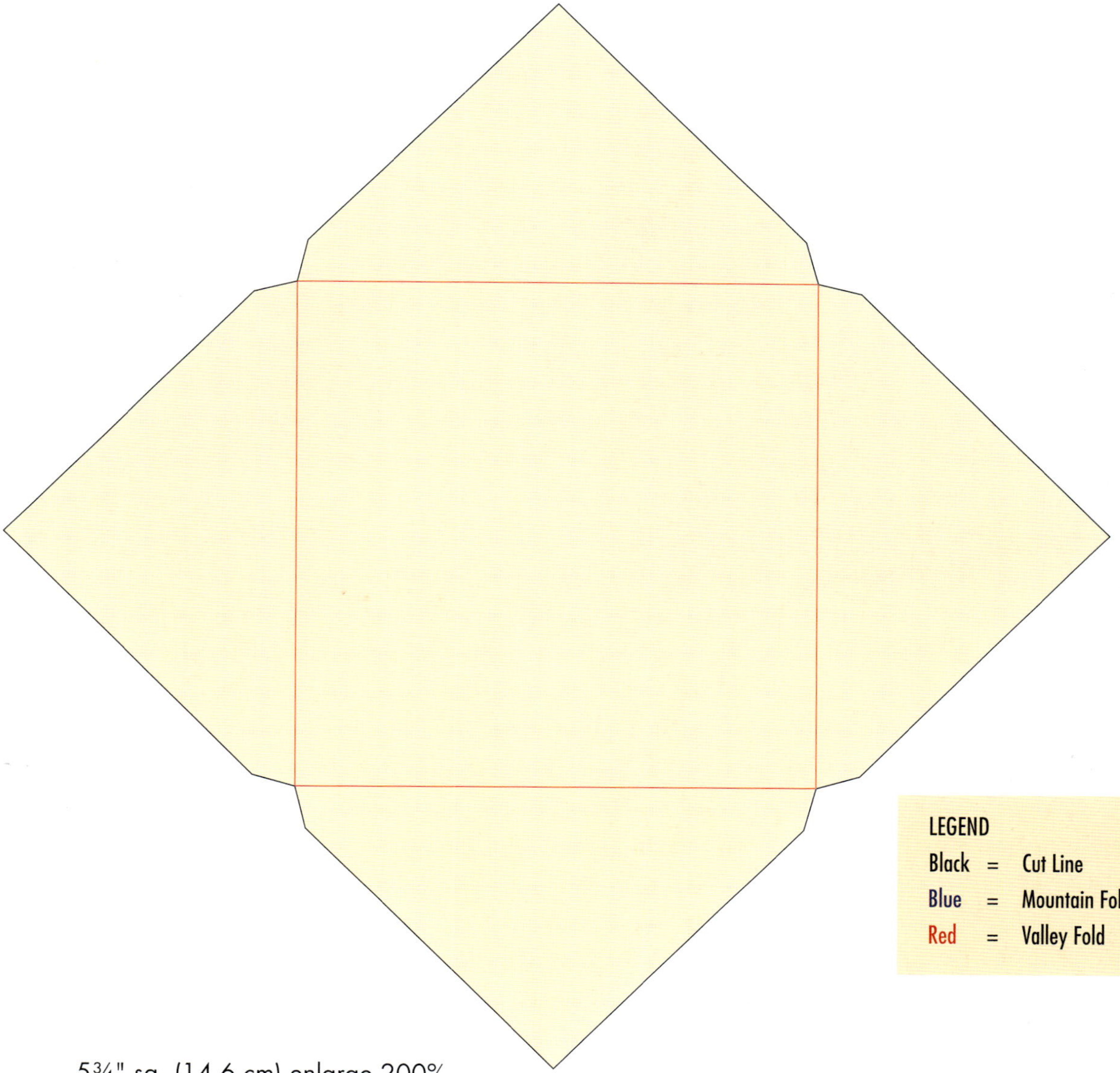

5¾" sq. (14.6 cm) enlarge 200%

LEGEND

Black	=	Cut Line
Blue	=	Mountain Fold
Red	=	Valley Fold

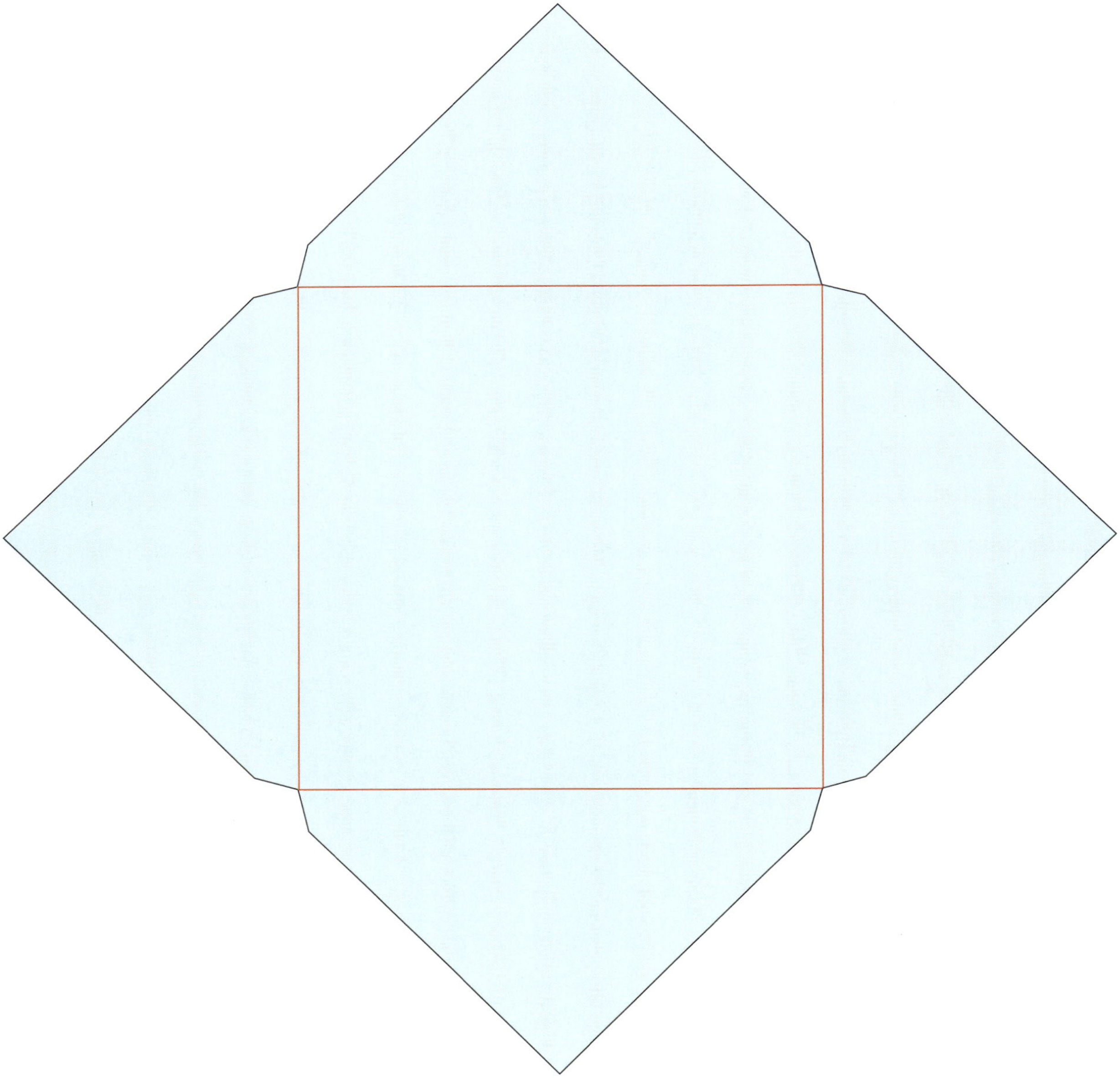

6" sq. (15.2 cm) enlarge 200%

8" sq. (20.3 cm) enlarge 275%

LEGEND

Black = Cut Line

Blue = Mountain Fold

Red = Valley Fold

6¼" x 8" (15.8 x 20.3 cm) enlarge 200%

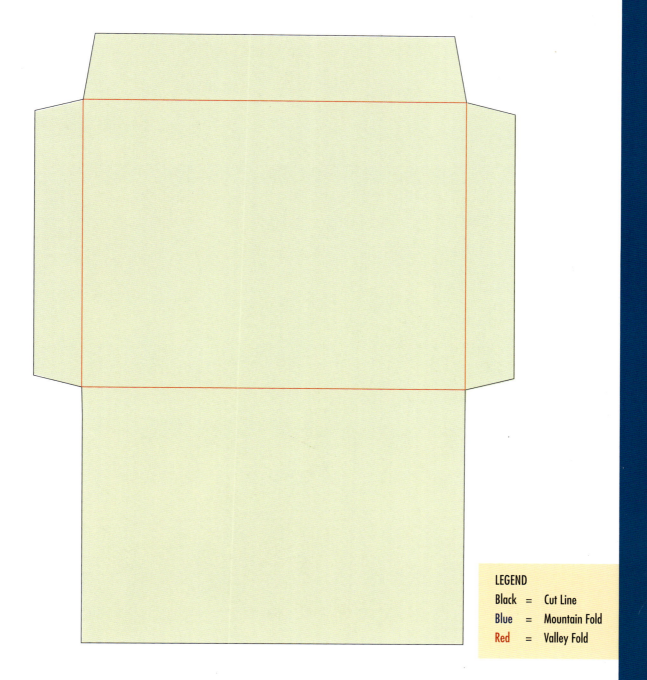

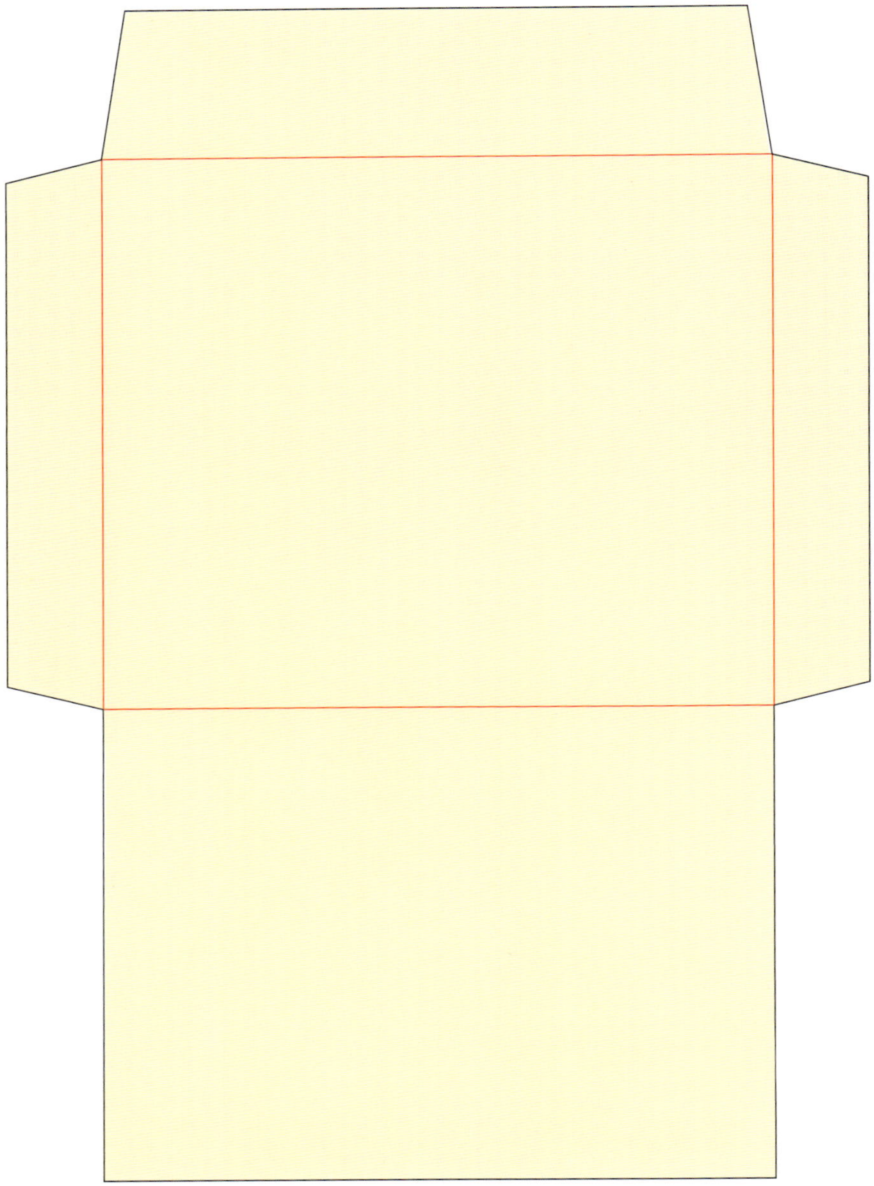

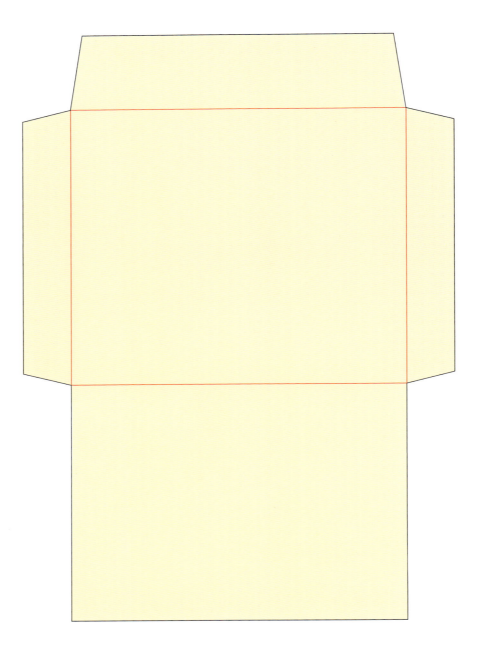

6" x 7" (15.2 x 17.8 cm) enlarge 200%

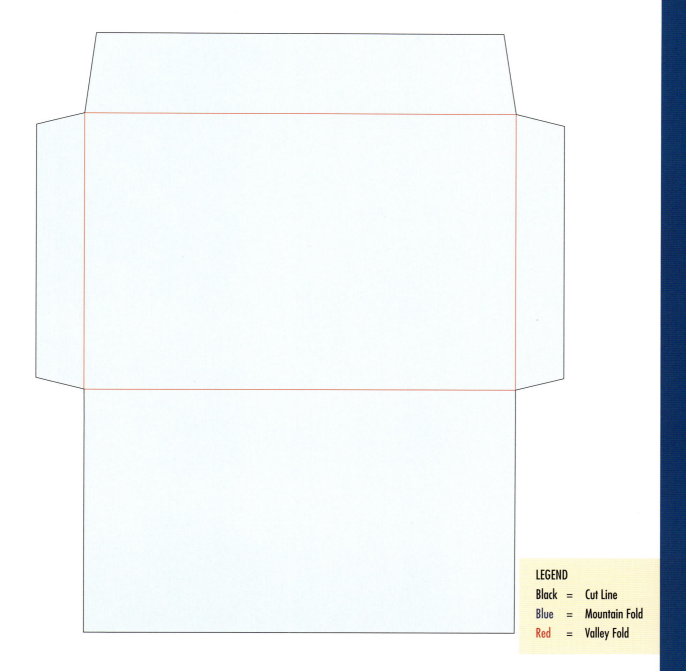

LEGEND

Black = Cut Line

Blue = Mountain Fold

Red = Valley Fold

A10 – 6" x 9" (15.2 x 22.9 cm) enlarge 200%

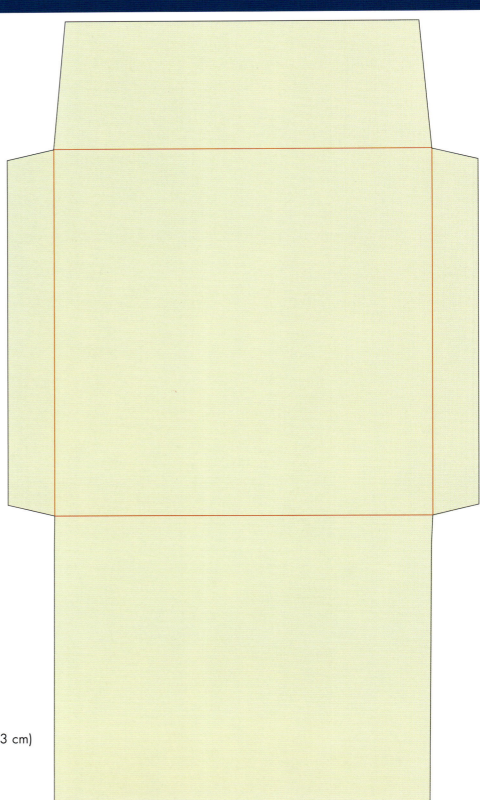

7⅝" x 8" (19.9 x 20.3 cm)

enlarge 200%

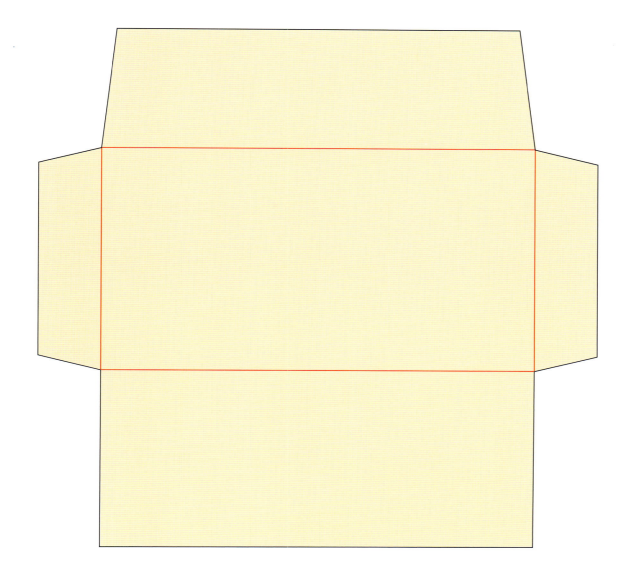

LEGEND

Black = Cut Line

Blue = Mountain Fold

Red = Valley Fold

3¾" x 7" (9.5 x 17.8 cm) enlarge 100%

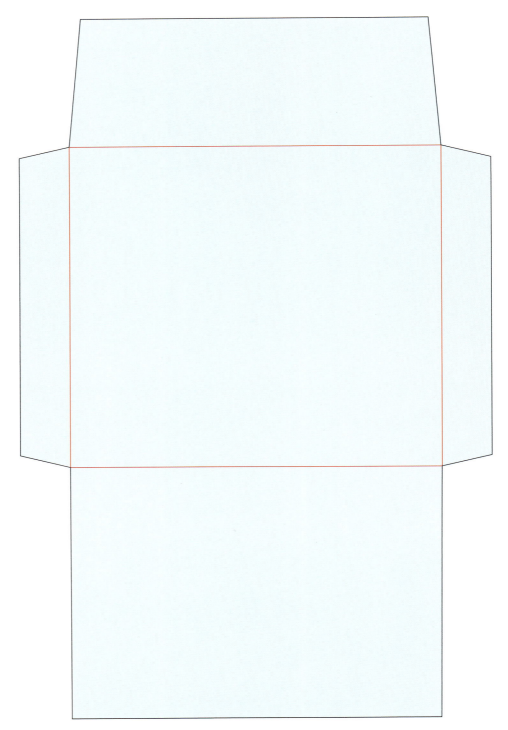

7¾" x 7" (19.7 x 17.8 cm) enlarge 200%

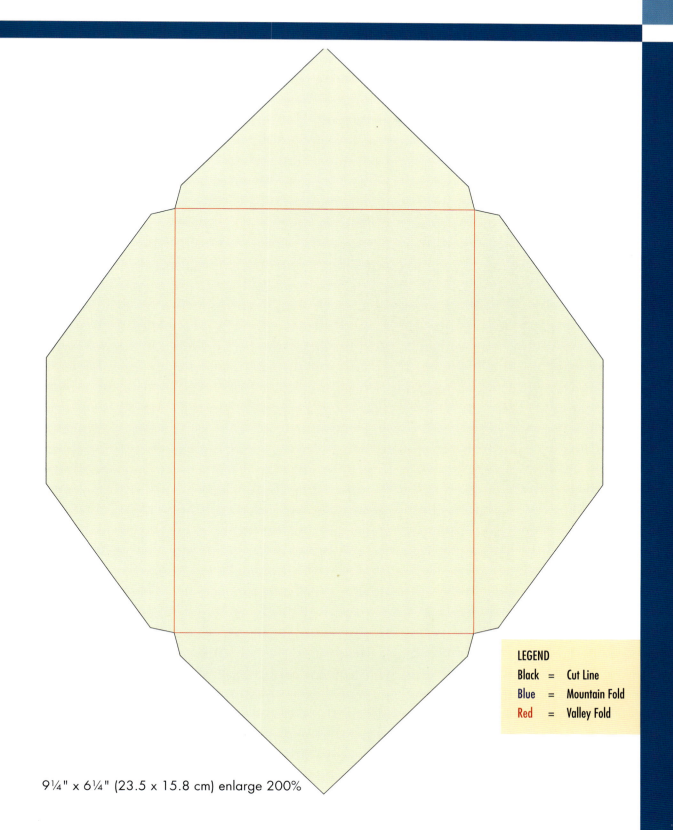

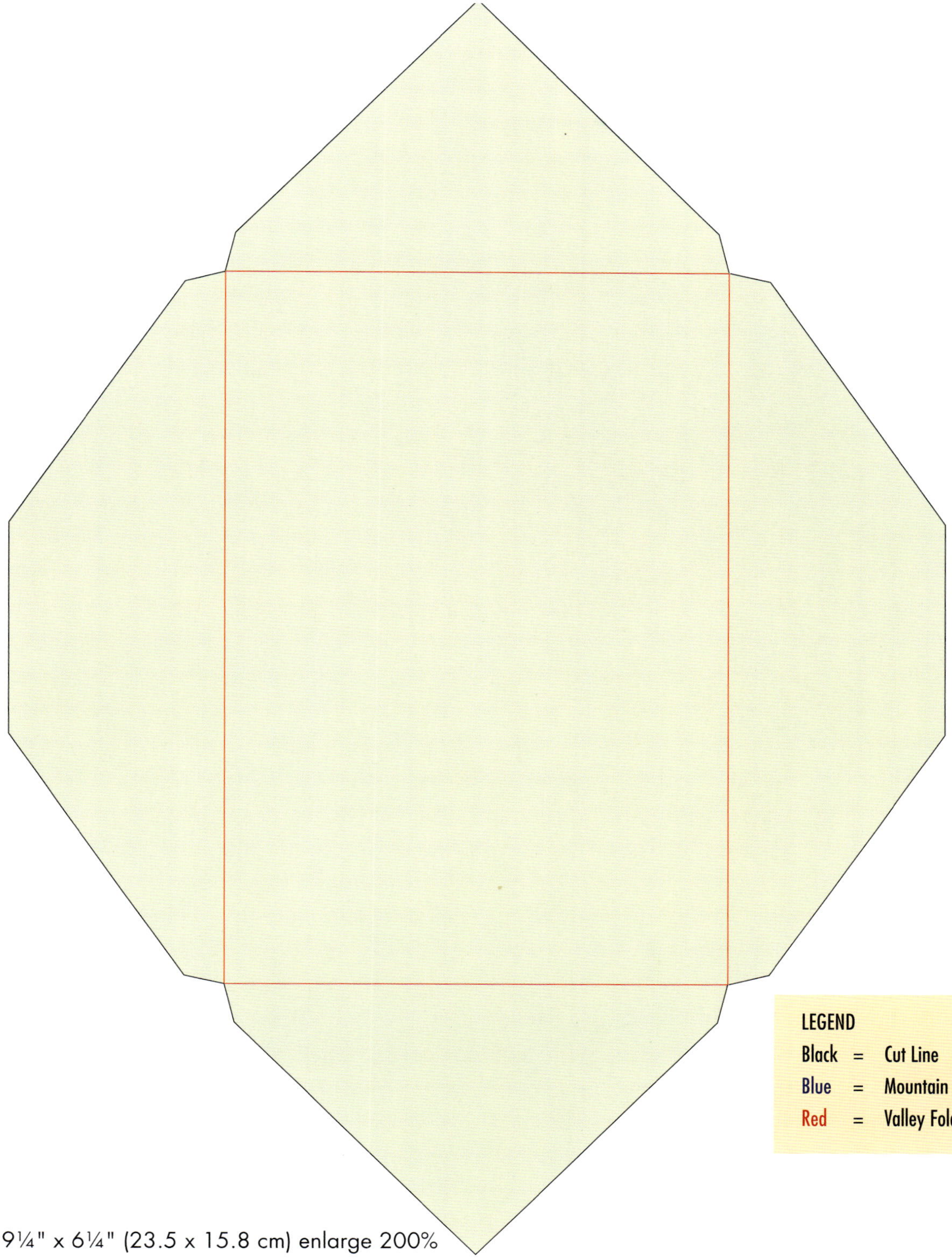

9¼" x 6¼" (23.5 x 15.8 cm) enlarge 200%

LEGEND

Black = Cut Line
Blue = Mountain Fold
Red = Valley Fold

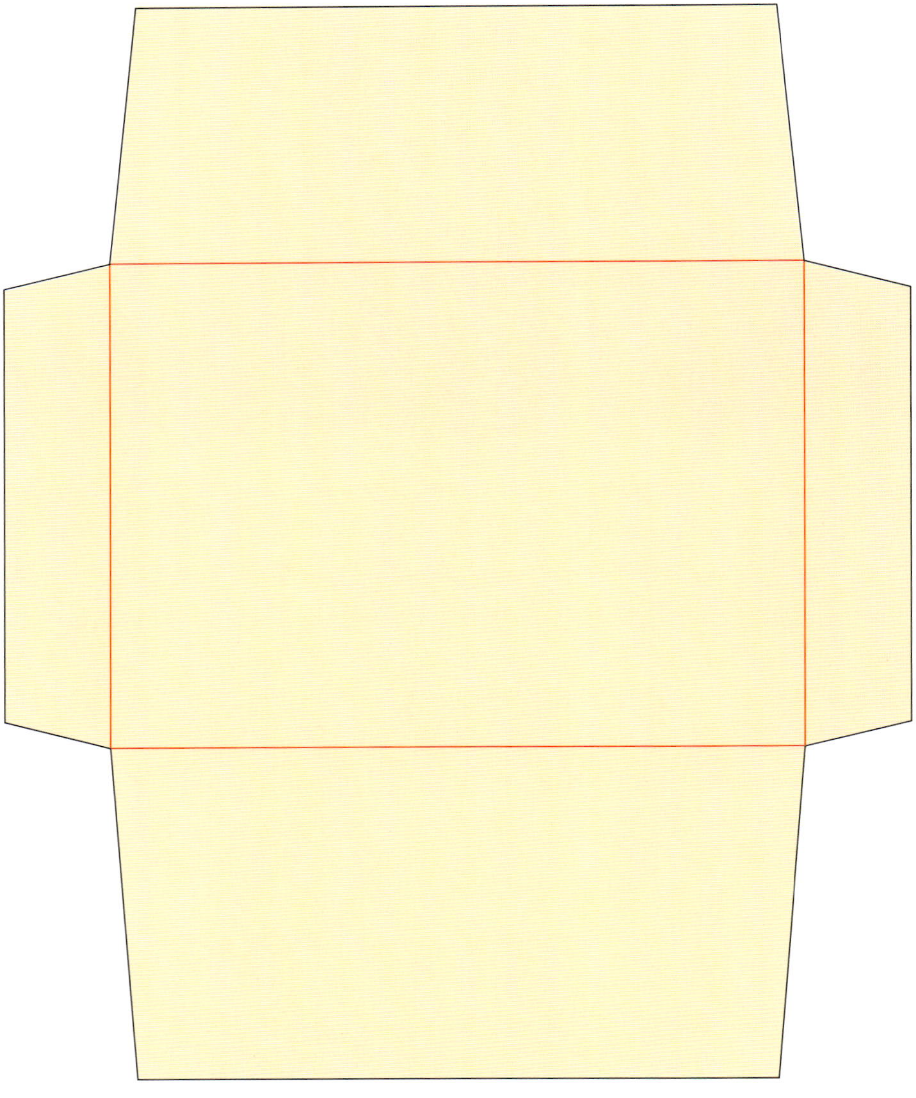

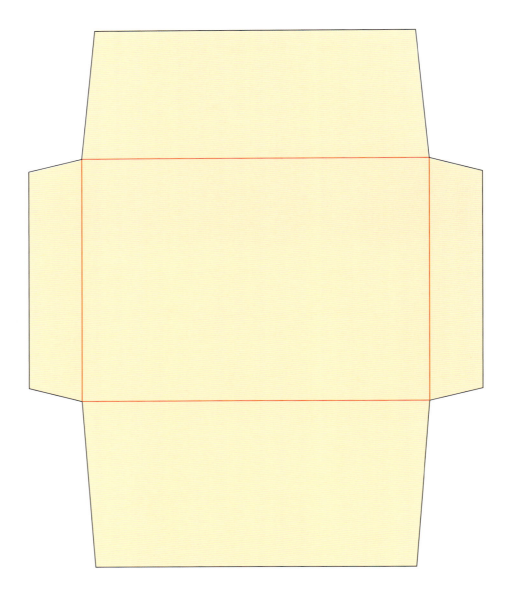

A6 – 4¾" x 6½" (12.1 x 17.6 cm) enlarge 175%

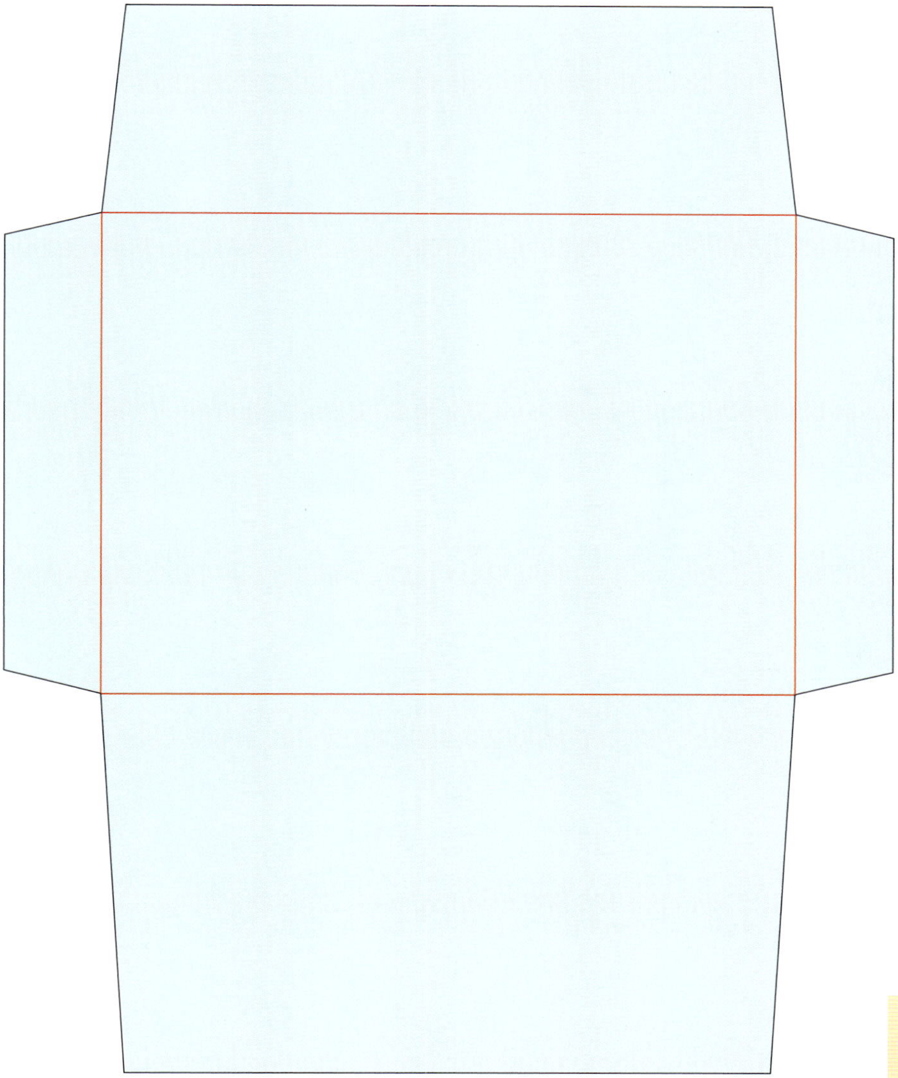

LEGEND

Black = Cut Line

Blue = Mountain Fold

Red = Valley Fold

A7 – 5¼" x 7¼" (13.3 x 18.4 cm) enlarge 200%

All About Sandi

Sandi Genovese is a multitalented author, artist, and educator who travels around the country demonstrating the latest in scrapbooking and paper crafting. She is the host of the popular *Scrapbooking* program airing weekdays on the DIY Network.

Sandi has been a spokesperson for various companies including Ellison, Nikon, and Kodak and writes a syndicated newspaper column. A frequent contributor to national magazines, she is also a familiar face to many viewers due to her numerous appearances on such television shows as *Good Morning America, The View, The Carol Duvall Show, Smart Solutions,* and *Home Matters* as well as on ABC, CBS, NBC, and Fox affiliates in cities across the country.

Sandi has developed crafting products, workshops, and die-cut designs for numerous companies, including Ellison, Sizzix, Mrs. Grossman's, and C.R. Gibson and she licenses pop-up scrapbooks and dimensional cards offered through QVC and Staples office supply stores. She shares her creativity in several books, including *Creative Scrapbooking, Creative Greeting Cards, Sandi Genovese's Three-Dimensional Scrapbooks* and *Designer Scrapbooks with Sandi Genovese* (also available on DVD). Sandi lives in Laguna Beach, California.

ACKNOWLEDGMENTS

I'd like to thank Mrs. Grossman's for their fabulous stickers, Canson for their beautiful oversized papers, Bazzill Basics for their wonderfully color-coordinated standard-sized papers, Ellison/Sizzix for their die cuts, and E.K. Success for their innovative paper punches and roller adhesive.

Index